The Only

POKER BOOK

You'll Ever Need

Bet, Play, and
Bluff Like a Pro

John "Johnny Quads" Wenzel

Adams Media
Avon, Massachusetts

Published by Adams Media, an F+W Publications Company
57 Littlefield Street
Avon, MA 02322
www.adamsmedia.com

ISBN: 1-59337-595-6

Printed in Canada.

J   I   H   G   F   E   D   C   B   A

Library of Congress Cataloging-in-Publication Data
Wenzel, John.
The only poker book you'll ever need / John "Johnny Quads" Wenzel.
p.   cm.
ISBN 1-59337-595-6
1. Poker. I. Title.
GV1251.W463 2006
795.412—dc22
2006005008

Contains portions of material adapted and abridged from *The Everything® Poker
Strategy Book* by John Wenzel, ©2004, F+W Publications, Inc.

This publication is designed to provide accurate and authoritative information
with regard to the subject matter covered. It is sold with the understanding that
the publisher is not engaged in rendering legal, accounting, or other professional advice. If legal advice or other expert assistance is required, the services
of a competent professional person should be sought.
  —From a *Declaration of Principles* jointly adopted by a Committee of the
American Bar Association and a Committee of Publishers and Associations

Many of the designations used by manufacturers and sellers to distinguish
their product are claimed as trademarks. Where those designations appear in
this book and Adams Media was aware of a trademark claim, the designations
have been printed with initial capital letters.

This book is available at quantity discounts for bulk purchases.
For information, please call 1-800-872-5627.

CONTENTS

INTRODUCTION

Welcome to poker! This game is filled with twists and turns, strategies and surprises. If you're new to the world of poker, get ready to be thrilled, challenged, and absorbed by this great game. If you've already experienced a few home games or have tried your hand at casino poker, this book will help you hone your skills and develop your strategies.

Poker players come in various shapes and sizes, but they all have a thing or two in common. From the days of the first poker mania when fancy gamblers preyed on river-boat rubes to today's high-tech hysteria fueled by television and the Internet, players have sought one thing: the secret to winning. Winning means money. Winning means fun. But winning consistently takes more than just buying some chips and getting a hand; otherwise, anyone with a buy-in and a pair of sunglasses would be rich. There is no magic formula, no recipe to follow.

Instead, you must watch and play and watch and play until your skills develop, putting big money at risk doesn't faze you, and your tablemates fear your unpredictable, unreadable style.

After reading the first few chapters of this book you'll probably be wondering, "Am I really ready to play?" This is a question too many players fail to ask. If you've had a few practice runs you'll probably know your skill level. But what players (even some very good ones) usually misjudge is their emotional readiness. You cannot play an intense game like poker, which requires focus and retention, if you are distracted. If you're worried about your girlfriend, boyfriend, spouse, job, the big loss you suffered yesterday, an argument, money problems, or anything that has you depressed or concerned, you will be off your game. When you sit down to a table you must be ready to focus, or you'll unintentionally offer your opponents countless chances to get the better of you.

Let this book be your personal guide as you navigate the stormy sea of poker—both in home games and at the casino. Not only will it teach you the essence and tactics of different variations, but it will also train you to read your opponents, perfect your table image, place bets with confidence, and rake in the pot. Everything you need to begin your poker adventure is right in front of you. So, what are you waiting for? Grab your cards and chips and turn the page!

CHAPTER 1

POKER 101

The well-worn cliché about poker says that "It is simple to learn, but it takes a lifetime to master." How true this is! Any intelligent person can learn the rules and the different hands in a few minutes, but the nuances and subtleties only become apparent over time. Your skills and strategies will keep evolving for as long as you play.

Your Poker Perspective

Each poker hand is its own battle, a skirmish in a larger game. Not just the game you're playing on a particular night—I mean the ongoing poker game you are playing throughout your entire life. You must think long-term. There will be games when no matter how well you play, you won't come out ahead. But if you play correctly, over time you will be a winner.

Don't let a few losing sessions or crazy hands tempt you to change your style. And don't be seduced by the "I would've won if I hadn't folded" refrain. Every good player has folded winning hands. It happens. You toss a trash Hold'em hand like 7-4 offsuit and get some crazy flop (like 7-7-4) that would have given you a full house. Your brain screams that you made a mistake, but you have to let it go. A miracle flop doesn't mean you should've called that bet. In fact, quite the opposite is true.

POKER POINTER

Many say that poker is "a people game played with cards, not a card game played by people." How you play a hand varies depending on who you're facing, the history of the game you're in, whether it is loose or tight, the stakes, and a host of other factors. Even Hold'em, which has only 169 possible starting hands, has infinite variations.

All poker discussions must by necessity be laden with "it depends." That's just the way it is. Relatives will try to pin you down on strategy. They'll ask stuff like, "What percentage of starting hands do you play?" and "Do you raise with small pairs?" You'll wrack your brain for a clever answer, but in the end you'll have to tell them, "It depends." Reading this book will help make the infinite more manageable for you—and the learning less expensive—but there is no magic potion that will turn you into a winner and no secret formula for playing hands. There is no substitute for experience.

Watch, Play, and Learn

Play, play, and play some more! Pay attention to every hand, even the ones you're not in. Watch the players—their mannerisms, their moves. Learn from the good players. Do you understand what a good hand is in the game you're playing? Do you know what a good hand is in particular situations in the game?

POKER POINTER

Play that is too conservative and cautious is called "tight" in poker circles, and tight players are derisively known as "rocks." Tight is a good way to start. You don't want to lose all your money playing questionable cards before you have learned the game. But good players don't always play tight. Tight is predictable, and being predictable is the surest way to lose a lot of money.

Rethink a hand after you've played it. When the game's over and you're back home, lying in bed, replay the game in your mind, every hand. And hang in there during your learning curve—everyone has some early losses. Here are some things to analyze later:

- How did you lose the most money?
- Who bluffed a lot, and who never did?
- How did that player who bluffed you out look and act during the hand?
- Were you too aggressive, or too timid?
- What type of hand made you the most money?

Again, you're going to have some losses, some bitter nights, especially early on. Even the very best, like Doyle Brunson and Daniel Negreanu, have gone broke at one time or another. But they learned. Today they are millionaires.

Here's the Deal

Poker uses a standard fifty-two-card deck. The cards have thirteen denominations and four suits: spades, hearts, diamonds, and clubs. Spades and clubs are black, and hearts and diamonds are red. The colors of the cards have no meaning in poker, and the suits have no rank: They are equal. Thus, if one player has an ace-high royal flush (A-K-Q-J-10) of hearts, and another has the same hand in spades, the pot is split. It is a tie.

The denominations, called ranks, from highest rank to lowest are as follows: ace, king, queen, jack, ten, nine, eight, seven, six, five, four, three, and two. Kings, queens, and jacks are called face cards because they are illustrated with pictures of characters. Some people call them "paints" because of their colorful inks.

The highest card is the ace, although in some lowball games—where the low hand wins—it is used as the lowest card in the deck (in other words, as a "one"). The ace can also always be used as a "one" to make a low straight (5-4-3-2-ace), known as a "wheel" or "bicycle."

POKER POINTER

Cards have pet names. A two is always referred to as a deuce, and a three is a trey. Queens are often called ladies, and kings are cowboys. Aces are colorfully termed "bullets," or, in Hold'em, a pair of aces in the hole are called "pocket rockets."

A session of poker consists of many hands, and you can gain or lose money in every hand. The object is to go home with more money than you came with. You win a poker hand by having more valuable cards than your opponents at the end of the hand. Players may drop out of a particular hand at any time. Once they drop out (called folding), they are out of that hand and do not figure in the outcome, even if they would have won had they not folded.

Curiously, the cards you hold during a particular hand are also called your "hand." All poker hands contain five cards. In games where you are dealt more than five cards, you may only use five cards to make your final hand. The other cards are not used, even in case of ties.

Give Yourself a Hand

The hardest hands to obtain have the greatest value. The most valuable hand—the "highest" hand—wins the hand and the pot (the money that has been wagered). The hands are presented here in descending order.

Royal Flush

This is a combination of both the highest straight (five cards in a row) and a flush (five cards of the same suit, whether spades, hearts, diamonds, or clubs). It is A-K-Q-J-10 of the same suit. Only four such hands exist, one for each suit. It is so rare you may never get one. Your chance of being dealt one of these in five cards is 1 in 649,740!

Straight Flush

A straight flush is five cards in a row (straight) all of the same suit (flush). It is identical to the royal flush except that the straight is *not* ace-high. A straight flush can be anything from king-high (K-Q-J-10-9) to five-high (5-4-3-2-A). The higher the first card of the straight flush, the better the hand. Thus, a king-high straight flush would beat a five-high. There are thirty-six straight flushes that are not royal. The chance of getting a straight flush is 1 in 72,193 in a five-card game with no draw.

Four of a Kind

Four of a kind is just what it says: four cards of identical rank, like four jacks or four deuces. The higher the rank of the card, the higher the hand. The best four of a kind is A-A-A-A. By holding four aces, you have every ace in the deck. Note that since poker is a five-card game, you will have an odd card that must complete the hand, so you might have A-A-A-A-5 or 9-9-9-9-K. This odd card, called a *kicker*, is used to break ties in poker, but since two four of a kinds can never tie (unless there are wild cards or community cards), the kicker here is irrelevant. Chance of being dealt a four of a kind: 1 in 4,165.

Full House

A full house is three cards of one rank and two of another. Suits do not matter. A full house can be A-A-A-K-K, the highest, all the way down to 2-2-2-3-3 (the lowest). When determining which full house wins (if there are more than one), the rank of the three identical cards is the determining factor. Thus, a full house of 9-9-9-2-2 beats a full house of 8-8-8-7-7. When describing your full house, you say "Full house, eights over sevens" or "Eights full of sevens" or just "Eights full." The chance of being dealt a full house in a five-card game is 1 in 694.

Flush

A flush is five cards of the same suit, like five hearts or five spades not in a row. If two players have flushes, the one with the highest card wins. (Suit does not matter.) An ace-high flush beats a king-high flush. A flush of Q-J-8-7-5 beats a flush of 10-9-6-5-3. You describe your hand as a "queen-high flush," or "flush, queen-high." If two players both have ace-high flushes, you go to the next card to determine the winner, all the way down to the fifth card, if necessary. So a flush of K-J-10-7-6 beats K-J-10-7-5. If all five cards are identical, then it is a tie and the pot is split. Chance of being dealt a flush: 1 in 509.

Straight

A straight is five cards in a row of mixed suits. For example, A-K-Q-J-10 or 9-8-7-6-5 or 6-5-4-3-2. The higher the straight, the better the hand. The high card in the straight determines its value. An ace-high straight is the highest. A 5-high straight (5-4-3-2-A) is the lowest. There is no such thing as an "around-the-corner straight" (J-Q-K-A-2). Chance of being dealt a straight in a five-card game: 1 in 255.

Three of a Kind

Three of a kind (also known as "trips") is three cards of the same rank, such as 8-8-8, and two unrelated cards, for a hand like 8-8-8-K-J. Suit is not a factor. Chance of being dealt a three of a kind in a five-card game: 1 in 47.

Two Pair

Two pair is, surprise, two pairs, and one unrelated card, for example, J-J-7-7-4. You have a pair of jacks and a pair of sevens. You say: "Two pair, jacks and sevens," or "Two pair, jacks up." The value of the hand is determined by the top pair. So J-J-2-2 beats 10-10-9-9. The lower pair is important only in case of a tie. For example, J-J-3-3 beats J-J-2-2. The kicker is also used for breaking ties when two players have two identical pairs. Example: J-J-3-3-9 beats J-J-3-3-8. Chance of two pair being dealt to you in a five-card game: 1 in 21.

One Pair

A pair is the most basic of poker hands, but it's also very important, for a pair gets you an early lead in many games that you can exploit. It also is a strong hand in Hold'em if your hole cards are a pair. In heads-up play (you against one other person), a pair is big, and it often takes the pot in Hold'em. If two players have the same pair, the other three cards determine the winner. Example: A-A-J-9-3 beats A-A-J-9-2. If two players have identical hands, the pot is split evenly. Chance of a pair on five cards: 1 in 2.37. That's a little less than one out of every two hands.

No Pair (High Card)

Half your hands will be no pair (nothing). This means you don't have a pair or anything ranked above it. The strength of the hand is determined by the high card. Example: A-J-9-8-2 of different suits is an "ace-high." 9-7-6-3-2 is a "nine-high." Ace-high beats nine-high. A-J-9-8-3 beats A-J-9-8-2. Identical hands split the pot (provided there isn't a better hand held by some other player, of course). Chance of being dealt nothing: about 50-50.

How to Play

Each poker hand is its own small game. The object of the game is to win the pot, which is all the money (or whatever you are playing for) that has been wagered and anted and placed in the center of the table. You win the pot by having the highest-ranking card hand out of all the players who have not dropped out (folded) and remain at the end of the hand. If only one person remains in the hand, and everyone else folds, he wins no matter what his hand is.

The winner is determined at the showdown, which begins after all remaining players have put their money in the pot in the final betting round. The last bettor turns over his hand first, followed by the remaining players, starting to his left and proceeding clockwise. The player who must show his hand first is *not* the last player to put chips in the pot. Rather, it is the last player who made a bet or a raise. (Players who match a bet are not betting; they are calling.)

The cards speak for themselves. A player may call his hand by saying "full house," for example, but if he has miscalled his hand, either high or low, it is the hand that counts, not what he says. If you called a hand "three eights" when you in fact had a full house and someone noticed it, you would get credit for the full house. You are not disqualified for miscalling.

After one of the final players has turned over a hand at the showdown, some other players may realize they are beat and concede the hand. They may then "muck" their cards, turning them over face down, not showing them and not contesting the pot. However, in casino play, anyone at the table has the right to see the hand of any player who called the final bet, just by requesting to see it. In home games, this is subject to house rule, so get it straight before the game starts. (The pile of discards, folded, and undealt cards is called the "muck." Thus we get the term "mucking.")

If only one person remains in the hand, that person wins the pot, regardless of what hand he has. This winning hand does *not* have to be shown, even if someone asks to see it. This is the origin of the phrase: "You want to see it, you pay for it." It is usually to your advantage not to show your hand.

After someone wins the pot, that person takes the money and a new hand begins.

Antes and Blinds

Blinds and antes get money in the pot so there is something to play for, and so players can't just sit and "play for free," waiting forever for a cinch hand. Antes are a fixed amount put in the pot by each player before the start of the deal, usually a percentage of the minimum bet. This gets a pot started. Most stud games and non–community-card games use antes.

ASK JOHNNY QUADS

Are both antes and blinds ever used in the same game?

In most Hold'em poker tournaments, when the limits get extremely high, there are blinds (two) and antes (everyone), so a large pot is out there right from the get-go. This leads to some frenetic final-table action.

Blinds are used in community-card games like Hold'em and Omaha. The small blind, located to the left of the dealer, puts half the minimum bet in the pot before the deal. The big blind, located to the left of the small blind, puts a full bet in the pot. This amounts to the big blind making a full bet "blind," without having seen his cards. After the deal, the action is on the player to the big blind's left. He must either call the big blind's "bet," fold, or raise. When the action comes back around to the small blind, he must complete his bet (put in the other half of this bet) and call any raises to stay in the hand for the next round. He also has the option of raising, as does the big blind, even if no one has raised him. On the next round, if they are still in the hand, the small blind will act first and the big blind second, but they are now just players like everyone else. Their role as blinds has ended.

Deal with It

In home games, except for the rare high-stakes ones that employ a house dealer, the deal rotates around the table in a clockwise direction, with each player getting a turn at dealing and, often, calling which game will be played. The dealer shuffles the deck three or four times, asks the player on his right to cut, and deals one card at a time. The player on his left is dealt first, and he deals himself last. Don't forget to offer a cut.

All play in poker goes in a clockwise direction, to the left. This includes dealing the cards, passing the deal, drawing cards, and betting. Players should always act in turn. The only thing done to the right is the cut of the cards.

When a professional dealer is used, as in a casino or serious home game, the deal still shifts around the table, even though no player ever actually deals. This is done by using a marker called the button. In casinos, it is a small, white plastic circle with the word "dealer" stamped on it. The button moves from player to player after each hand. The player "on the button" has the best seat in the house, because in many games, like Hold'em and Omaha, he is the last to act on every round, just as if he were actually dealing the cards.

POKER POINTER

A misdeal occurs when the dealer accidentally turns one or more of a player's hole (hidden) cards face up, thus exposing it to another player. Misdeals also occur if someone is dealt too many or too few cards, players are dealt in the wrong order, or any situation where the normal order of the cards is disrupted. Handling of a misdeal is subject to house rule.

The dealer uses the button to determine where to begin dealing. Since the player on the button is the "dealer," the cards are dealt to the player on his left first. The deal then proceeds clockwise, ending with the player on the button. After the hand, the button moves to the left, and the player who acted first now is the "dealer" and acts last during the next hand.

Placing Bets

The prize in every poker hand is the pot, but where does it come from? You know about the blinds and antes. But that's just a start. When the action is on a player (that is, it's his turn to act), that player has the option of checking, betting, or folding. The pot is built through bets. A bet is how a player maximizes his profit on a hand, or at least presses a perceived advantage. To bet, he says, "Bet" or just puts money in the pot, within the limits of the game.

To fold (or quit the hand), a player simply says "fold," turns his hand over, and gives it to the dealer. If he is first to act, he should never fold. The only time a player should fold is if another player has bet and he does not want to call (match the bet, also known as "seeing," back in the day). If there is no bet for him to call, and he does not wish to bet himself, he can pass by just saying "check" or rapping the table. He is still in the hand, but has chosen not to bet. If someone has bet, other players must match the bet or give up the hand.

POKER POINTER

If everyone checks, play proceeds to the next round, where players will receive their next card "free." No matter how poor your hand is, don't throw it away until someone forces you to act by betting. The free card could change everything!

Betting Rounds

As soon as any player makes a bet, the option to check becomes unavailable, but a new option appears, the raise. Now you can either fold, call the bet, or raise. By folding, you are out of the hand. By calling, you are in the hand as long as no one raises. By raising, you increase the amount a player must pay to stay in the game and go on to the next round. To raise, you say "Raise" and put in the amount of all bets made so far, plus the amount of your increase (your raise). Just keep in mind that you cannot raise less than the amount the other player bet. If it's a $5 bet to you, and you raise, you would put in $10. Other players now have to match $10. If someone reraises (raises the raiser), he would put in $15 (unless larger bets are allowed). If that happens, you have another decision to make—call, fold, or raise, the same choices you had the first time around. This continues until all players have either called all raises or folded. The betting round is now over.

There are limits on the number of raises allowed per round in almost all casino and home games. This is to protect a player from being "whipsawed" between two raising players (sometimes in collusion) to the point where he must fold or pour all his money in the pot. Most casinos limit raises to three or four per round. That's *raises,* not total bets. A bet and four raises makes five total bets.

POKER POINTER

Note that if you are heads-up (just two players left) in many casino games, and the round of betting began with just two players, there is no limit on the number of raises.

Betting Limits

Virtually all games have betting limits to keep the stakes at a desired level. In standard two-tiered limits, designated as $5–$10 or $10–$20 (and so on), players can only bet those specific amounts. In early rounds in a $5–$10 game, players can bet or raise only $5. In later rounds, they can only bet or raise in increments of $10. There are no other choices. In games like $2–$10, common for Stud, a player can bet any-where from $2 to $10 any time. *No-limit* poker is just what it says: You can bet any amount you have in front of you at any time. In *pot-limit*, you can bet an amount up to the size of the pot any time. In pot-limit, your call is considered part of the pot. For example, if the pot is $10, and someone raises the pot size, there is now $20 in the pot. If you want to raise, you first call the bet ($10), making the pot $30. You can now raise up to $30, for a possible $60 pot, $40 of which is your money.

Table Stakes

No matter what limit you play, in all casino and most home games, table stakes are used. That means a player can't bet more money than he has on the table. Once a player has put all the money he has on the table into the pot, he announces "all-in," and if it's a heads-up game (just two play-ers), the betting stops. No one can risk more than he has in front of him; players cannot dig into their pockets for more, borrow money, or hand out checks or IOUs during a hand. Once someone is all-in, the opponent equals the all-in amount (if he chooses to call), and the betting is over. If it is the last round, players just turn their cards up and the win-ner takes the pot. If there are more than two players involved, the ones with money remaining can still bet. Their chips go in a side pot. The "all-in" player is only eligible for the main pot, but the other players are eligible for both pots.

Which Game to Play?

By far the most popular poker games today are Texas Hold'em, Seven-Card Stud, and Omaha. The rules for these games are universal throughout the world and are briefly presented in this section to get you started.

Texas Hold'em

Texas Hold'em is a seven-card game with two hole cards, five community (shared) cards, and two blind bets. Hold'em generally uses a two-tiered betting structure with four betting rounds. The first two rounds use what's called a small bet. The second two rounds use a bet twice that size, termed a big bet.

For example, if the limits are $5–$10, $5 is the only bet allowed during the first two rounds, with the designated number of raises, and in the second two rounds, there's a $10 betting limit. In most such games, $5 and $10 are the only bets allowed during their rounds, with nothing in between. There are no $2, or $4, or $7 bets, for example.

POKER POINTER

Even if the big blind's initial "automatic bet" has only been called, both blinds still have the option of raising, since they are "live." For example, in a $4–$8 game, if the big blind is $4, the small blind is $2, and two players call, the small blind can raise by adding another $6. The big blind can raise by adding $4.

To begin, each player is dealt two cards face down, after which a round of betting ensues, with the player to the left of the big blind acting first, and the action then proceeding clockwise. Since the big blind is a bet, the player next to him must match that bet (call), fold, or raise. Other players then have the same option. When the action returns to the blinds, they can call bets as necessary, fold, or raise.

When that first round is completed, the dealer places the "flop" in the center of the table. The flop is three face-up community cards shared by all players. Another betting round ensues. The dealer then turns a fourth card face up, called the "turn," followed by another betting round. Then the dealer turns up the fifth and final community card, called the "river." There is one last round of betting, then the show-down.

There are now five community cards all players can use to make their five-card poker hand. A player may utilize all five cards on the board, or may choose to use four board cards and one from his hand or three board cards and both his hole cards. High hand wins.

Seven-Card Stud

Seven-Card Stud, known simply as "Stud," is a seven-card game with three hole cards and four up cards. There are no shared cards. Stud uses antes, not blinds. The antes are a fraction of the first bet and are put in the pot by all players prior to the deal. There are casino games, $1–$5 limit, for example, where the ante is as low as a dime. Some may have no ante at all. A dollar would be considered a high ante (in a $1–$5 game) but is great for a home game. The higher the ante, the more action.

The first round of betting comes after players are dealt two hole cards and one face-up card. In home games, the person with the highest card showing has the option of betting first. Sometimes the bet is mandatory, and it must be for at least the minimum allowable bet. In a casino, to build a pot, the low card "brings it in." In a $1–$5 game, for example, the bring-in might be a dollar, a quarter, or fifty cents, depending on the casino. This is the only time a bet can be for less than the minimum.

POKER POINTER

Some Stud games are played with a "spread limit." In $1–$5 Stud, for example, a player can bet as little as a buck or as much as $5 at any time, or any amount in between, such as $2, $3, or $4. The only stipulation is that raises must be for at least the amount of the original bet. If someone raises you $5, you cannot then reraise him $2.

If the high card brings it in, and two players both have the top card (like each showing an ace), then the suit of the high card (spades highest, then hearts, diamonds, and clubs) determines who acts first. This is true for later rounds as well, if two players have identical up cards that are high on the board. In casinos where low card brings it in, suit is used to settle ties, with clubs being lowest, then diamonds, hearts, and spades.

After the first round of betting, the dealer gives remaining players a second face-up card. This is the fourth card dealt, known as fourth street. (A street is the cards dealt on a particular round: the fourth card is known as fourth street; the fifth card is fifth street.) It is followed by another betting round. On fourth and remaining streets, the high hand showing on board acts first.

Another up card comes on fifth street, followed by a betting round. A sixth card, also up, is dealt on sixth street, then another betting round. On seventh street, players are dealt their last hole card, followed by the last betting round. High hand on board still acts first. The showdown follows, where players make their best five-card hand. (The two extra cards are not used—even to break ties.) In Stud games using a two-tiered limit, like $5–$10, the low limit is in effect for the first two rounds, the higher limit for the final three.

Omaha High

Omaha is the most intense and unpredictable of the "big three" casino poker games. It will test your courage—and your bankroll. The game is played like Hold'em but with four hole cards instead of two. With a total of nine cards to choose from, anything can happen—and usually does. The catch is that you must use two hole cards to complete your hand. No more, no less. So a player could have four eights in the pocket, but he only has two eights to work with—he'll never even make trips. And if he has four cards to a flush, he really only has two—and the two extra flush cards actually hurt him, because that's two more cards to the suit that will never appear on the board. If your hole cards are two pair, you don't have two pair—you have one pair plus three cards on the board.

It is often difficult, especially for new players, to figure out exactly what their hand is in Omaha—especially in the high-low variation. Even if you think you've lost, turn your hand face up at the showdown and let the dealer call your hand. While he's reading it, double-check it yourself to make sure he's right.

Omaha Eight or Better

This high-low split game (written as "Omaha 8/B") is actually more popular than straight Omaha. The games are identical, except that a qualifying low hand (five cards eight-or-below unpaired) takes half the pot. Cards speak, and straights and flushes don't count against the low. Ace is the lowest card in a low hand, the highest in a high hand. Different hole cards may be used to make high and low hands. Because of the "must use two hole cards" rule, there must be three cards eight or below on the board for a qualifying low to be possible.

POKER POINTER

Unlike in Hold'em, where you shouldn't fear that someone has the nuts (best possible hand) against you, in Omaha, someone almost always has it.

Low hands are "read" from high to low. An 8-6-4-3-2 is termed an "eight-low" or "eight-six" or "eighty-six." The 8-6-4-3-2 would beat 8-7-4-3-A, because the six is lower than the seven. Omaha 8/B can be a real action game, with many players seeing the flop and overflowing pots.

If you have four unpaired low cards in your hand, your chance of making a low is 49 percent. If two low cards flop, your chance increases to 70 percent, but if only one low card hits, your chance is down to 24 percent.

CHAPTER 2

GET THE ODDS
ON YOUR SIDE

I n poker conversation, you may have heard the statement, "It's all luck." But nothing could be further from the truth. What is termed "luck" can be a critical factor during a particular hand, even a particular week or month. On the other hand, the players who believe "luck" will bail them out are the ones who soon find their money in the pockets of those who don't.

Count on Your Skills, Not Luck

The beauty of poker is that you are playing against people—not an unrelenting roulette wheel or slot machine. Your opponents make decisions, many of them wrong. And more than in any other game, you can make your own decisions, too—sound, logical decisions based on reasoning and psychology.

If you sit down at a Hold'em table with nine others, your odds of ending up big winner are *not* 9-to-1! Your chances are determined by how much better or worse you are than these people. If you're a lot more skilled, your odds could be just 5-to-1, 3-to-1 or perhaps as good as 1-to-1 (even money), given enough playing time. If you're playing against world champs, on the other hand, the odds might be 100-to-1 against you.

POKER POINTER

Over time, you will get about the same number of good and bad hands as anyone else. It's how you play them that will determine your fortunes, not Lady Luck. Calling luck a "lady" leads people to believe luck is something tangible, when it doesn't exist at all.

Good poker players don't resort to superstition or "luck" because they are not gamblers, any more than a casino is gambling when it sets up a craps table and has a guaranteed advantage on every bet. Take this example. Daredevil Robbie Knievel is going to jump a motorcycle over a row of umpteen buses. Looks like he'll kill himself, you say. Well, if *you* tried it, not having a clue about how to do it, you would indeed be "lucky" if you survived. It's a pure gamble, a roll of the dice. But for Robbie—who has studied speed and distance and wind and knows his bike and has done it many times—while there is still danger, a whole lot of things would have to go wrong for him *not* to clear those buses. For him, it's not a gamble; it's a calculated risk, a small one. He knows he'll make it close to 100 percent of the time.

And that should be *you* at the poker table if you are to be successful. You won't clear those buses every time (win every game), but when you know what you are doing, you will be taking a calculated risk, not a gamble, and that risk will be minuscule. Once you're a knowledgeable player, you can get the math on your side, and a lot of bad things have to happen for you to lose money, even short-term.

How to Make Money at Poker

You aren't going to win every hand, nor should you try to. You make as much money from folding at the right time as

Here's how you win:

- Make more with your good hands. Bet it up with the lead, and make others pay to catch up.
- Don't get "married" to a hand. Fold when it's obvious you're facing superior cards.
- Don't feel you have to "protect" chips. Chips you've already tossed into the pot are no longer yours.
- Don't play marginal hands. Be patient.
- Be unpredictable. Vary your play. Bluff once in awhile to keep them guessing.
- Be friendly. You don't want to make enemies at the table.
- Be fearless and (selectively) aggressive. Play at a limit comfortable for you, uncomfortable for others.
- Adapt your style to the type of game (mild or wild, and so on) you're in and the players you are facing.

Looking for the opposite of these qualities is a good way to spot weaker players.

you do from raking pots. Pros pride themselves on what they call good folds, or "good laydowns." They know that money saved is the same as money won. It may sound obvious, but you win by being a better player than your opponents. Know more about the game and the odds; be more observant, focused, and patient; and keep improving your skills.

Psychological Versus Mathematical

Expert poker players have two main sets of skills: the psychological and the mathematical. The psychological enables you to find patterns and weakness in your opponents and divine their hands; the mathematical helps you decide your chance of winning, and therefore how much money to invest. The mathematical cannot alone make you into a champion player, but without understanding probability you will be lost.

Mathematical Players

Players who rely on odds alone are never top players, but they don't lose much, either. The math can help you when all else fails, like when you don't have a read on someone or when you're on a draw and don't know whether to try to chase someone down. The paradox of probability in its purest form is that it can tell you with mathematical certainty what will happen *over time*, like how often you'll make your flush draw or inside straight, but it cannot tell you if you'll make it *this time*.

It is the dream of the mathematical players that they can use probability to make the correct decision on every hand. Alas, they often can't do this without knowing everyone else's cards (and in some cases, using a computer). Thankfully, most math-oriented players aren't as good at reading people, betting, or playing fearlessly as they are at figuring odds, or we'd all be in trouble.

Anti-Gamblers

"Percentage players" are like anti-gamblers. While gamblers will play hunches and streaks, math guys seek to only bet when they have a mathematical advantage. For example, the Gambler says he'll pull an ace out of the deck, but wants odds. The Numbers guy thinks: "There are 52 cards and 4 aces. His probability is 4 out of 52, or 1 out of 13. So correct odds are 12-to-1. On average, he'll hit once for every twelve losses. If I give him 12-to-1 for $100 a pop, he'll lose twelve times for $1,200, but then get $1,200 for his win. It's a tie. But I'll come out ahead if I offer him only 11-to-1," the Numbers guy ponders, "and only have to pay him $1,100 when he wins, so I'll have $100 profit. I've got the best of it!" The Gambler, who may or may not know the real odds, takes the 11-to-1 because he's *sure* he'll pull that ace out, but of course, unless he is clairvoyant, he's going to lose, over time, $100 to the Numbers guy for every thirteen times he pulls a card. It's a bad bet.

ASK JOHNNY QUADS

How might the Gambler win over the short term?

He pulls six cards, no ace, and loses $600. He finds an ace on the seventh try and wins $1,100. He's won $500, if he walks away. Do you know any gamblers who would walk away? Didn't think so, but the math guys would walk. Except that they wouldn't have taken the worst of it in the first place, would they?

The Gambler might do all right at poker, though, when he drives the predictable math major out of pot after pot. At poker, percentage players can get killed by streaky, fearless players, especially over the short term. The Numbers guys go through horrible times where the gods of math seem to have deserted them. The good ones take comfort in the long term and stay the course, waiting for the deviation to approach the midpoint.

Figure Out Your "Outs"

During play, while your hand is still building, it only has potential. You either want your cards to be the best at every point in the hand (in which case you will often be betting like crazy), or you want them to have the potential to be the best hand at the end (in which case you *might* bet). The probability that yours will be best, as well as your payoff if you make it, determines whether that hand should be played.

POKER POINTER

If someone says you have a 10 percent chance it means you have 90 percent against you. The probability is 10 out of 100, so the odds are 90-to-10 against you, which simplified is 9-1 against. At 25 percent (25 out of 100), your odds are 3-1 against. At 50 percent (50 out of 100), your chance is 50-50, also called 1-to-1 odds or even money.

Every hand has a value, and you want to play hands that have the expectation of making you money over time. You don't play hands that will lose money. You'll learn good from bad by reading and playing, but good and bad are relative only to earning power. An A-K will win 41 percent of the time against four random hands going to the river, while Q-2 is only 20 percent. Still, poker being *situational*, there are times when you could bet, and win, with that Q-2, even against A-K! But you don't want to be on the chasing side of the odds if you don't have to be. You want to be the favorite and to bet it up in lower-limit games. The lower the limit, the more necessary it is that you have a real hand, rather than just skills, to win.

Sometimes odds can be difficult to figure, not because of the math involved, but because you're not sure what your opponents are holding. It is this uncertainty that makes poker interesting. As you progress, you'll get better at "putting people on hands," and this will make it easier to figure your odds of winning.

How to Calculate "Outs"

Poker players think in terms of "outs"—the number of cards left in the deck that will make your winning hand. If someone is chasing *you*, you're calculating how many outs *he* has so you can discover *his* chance of making his hand and beating *you*. You then compare the outs to the number of unseen cards in the deck to find the odds.

Say there's one card to come in Hold'em, you have pocket kings, and the board is Q-Q-7-2 rainbow (that is, different suits). You figure someone has a queen in the hole for trip queens. The only way you win is if a king comes. There are two left in the deck. (Yes, it's possible someone might have folded a king, but when figuring outs you must use *all* unseen cards, because you just don't know.) So you have two outs. There are only six seen cards: your two kings and the four board cards. Subtracting six from fifty-two leaves forty-six.

Your probability is 2 out of 46, which is the same as 1 out of 23. You'll make your hand once in twenty-three tries. This makes your odds 22-to-1, or a true longshot. (If you're interested in percentages, divide 2 by 46 [or 1 by 23], and you arrive at 4.3 percent. You will make this draw only about four times out of a hundred tries!)

Hold'em Example

Here's another Hold'em scenario. You have pocket aces. The board is A-6-7-10, all spades. You're sure that at least one of your two remaining foes has a spade for an ace-high flush. There's a bet to you. Do you call? An aces-over full house would be a guaranteed winner. What is your chance of making it? (Actually, someone with trip sixes, sevens, or tens could make four of a kind to beat you. What is the chance of that? Subtract the known cards—four on board, two in his hand, and two in your hand—from fifty-two, and you get forty-four unknown cards. There is one card that would make quads, so his odds are 43 to 1—so remote as to be discounted. You're just going to assume no one's going to make quads.)

ASK JOHNNY QUADS

How are odds and probability differentiated?

The probability of pulling a specific card, like the ace of spades, out of a fifty-two-card deck is 1 in 52 because there is one correct event out of fifty-two possible outcomes. There's 1 chance for, 51 against. In odds form, that's stated as "51-to-1 against" or "51-1 against."

Back to your problem: whether to call. First of all, you're drawing to the winning hand. You shouldn't draw to hands that might end up second-best even if you hit it. Second, how many outs do you have? You have one ace (to hit quads) and three sixes, three sevens, and three tens that will make your full house. That's ten outs out of an unseen deck of forty-six cards (you've subtracted the board and your two aces from fifty-two). The odds against you are 36-to-10. Simplified, that's 3.6-to-1. Not bad, especially since there's a nice pot built up.

But wait. If you are *sure* that an opponent has a set (trips) of sixes, sevens, or tens, then you have to subtract three cards from your outs and two from the unseen cards. (That's two from the pair in his hand that can't help you make your full house, and the fourth card of that rank that is in the deck and no longer an "out" because it would give him quads.) Now your odds are 37-to-7, or 5-to-1. (You get 5-to-1 by dividing 7 outs into the 44. You arrive at 6.3, which you round to 6, more than close enough. You have 1 chance in 6, so your odds are 5-to-1.) This is getting to be a longshot.

Pot Odds to the Rescue

Is it ever "right" to go for a draw, to chase a card, to go for a longshot? Even the percentage players would answer this with a resounding "Yes!" And the reason is something that pros have known for years: pot odds.

When you use pot odds, you are simplifying a difficult decision by turning it into a standard proposition bet, like the Gambler and Numbers guy did when they bet on pulling an ace out of the deck. You compare how much it will cost you to call against how much is in the pot, and you can quickly see if you are getting a fair return. In the above Hold'em example, you are getting 5-to-1 to make aces full and win. Say the game's $10–$20 and it's going to cost you $20 to call. Sounds steep, considering you'll only hit the hand once every six tries. But then you look at the pot. There's at least $150 in there! The pot is laying you 150-20, or 7.5-to-1 odds, 50 percent better than the correct 5-to-1. So you definitely call.

POKER POINTER

Taking less than proper odds from the pot is no different than going to the track and taking 3-1 odds on a horse that should be a 6-1 longshot. You'll be out of money very quickly, always taking the worst of it. Treat the pot as a bookie, and get better than correct odds, or don't bet.

Think about it: Over many similar situations, you will lose your $20 five times for a total of $100, but you'll win one time for $150. You're up $50 for every six occurrences, on average! This is the elusive edge top players try to achieve on every hand. While you are a big underdog to hit your hand, the pot odds give you the best of it over time.

Using Pot Odds Before the River

Using pot odds prior to the river is a little trickier. First of all, it's harder to be sure that the hand you're drawing to will be unbeatable at the showdown. If you're not drawing to the nut hand, that changes your odds completely because you have to allow for times when you will hit your hand and don't win. Pot odds become a much less useful tool if you can be beat, so much so that they often can't be used. If you are going to pour money in on a longshot, make sure it is a winner. If you're chasing a straight and there's a flush draw present, that is not a nut draw. If you are seeking a flush and the board pairs, someone might have a full house, so that is not a nut draw.

If there's more than one card to come, pot odds must be figured one card at a time. Say you're playing $10–$20 Hold'em with A-J, both spades, and the flop is 10♠, 6♠, and 5♥. There are four of you in the pot, and it's $10 to you. You have a nut flush draw. You get excited because you know you have a better than 2-to-1 chance of hitting it by the river. You think the nut flush will be a sure winner. But you have forgotten that unless you're going all-in, you will face a bet on the turn also. When figuring pot odds, you have to use your chances of making your hand *on the next card only*. The bet after the turn will entail a different set of odds. There's now $50 in the pot, your odds of hitting the flush *on the turn* are 4-1 (9 out of 47). You're getting 5-1 from the pot, so you can justify a call, but everyone else folds. Not good. Now you're stuck chasing against one player.

ASK JOHNNY QUADS

Should I keep track of how much is in the pot?

Yes, so you can quickly figure pot odds. An easy way is to total it up in terms of "small bets" on early streets, "big bets" later on.

The deuce of diamonds hits on the turn, and your opponent bets $20, which makes the pot $80. You're getting 4-1, a borderline call, but you grudgingly do. (For the record, a 4-1 shot is a 20 percent chance, 1 in 5. Your chance of rivering the flush is 19.6 percent.) The pot is now $100, but $40 of it was yours. You could make your hand on the river, bet, your opponent then folds, and you've risked $40 on a drawing hand just to win $60! Pot odds before the river can be a risky proposition. Too many players use it to justify throwing in money on longshots.

The river is the five of spades. You hit it! Now three scenarios could occur. One, you bet and he folds, having correctly figured you for a flush. Two, you bet and he calls to keep you honest. Three, he makes a full house on the river. He bets, you raise, he reraises, pushing your total loss on the hand to $100. He had flopped a set of tens and now has tens full of fives. Where you went wrong was figuring your outs. You didn't have nine spade outs—you had seven. The five and deuce of spades were not outs, as they gave him a full house. So your odds were 5-1, not 4-1, and they were not good enough to call.

POKER POINTER

Don't chase draws against just one player. First of all, you will rarely get proper pot odds to call. Second, if you hit a draw, like a flush or a straight, you want a big payoff to make up for all the times you missed. If you must chase, wait for a larger field.

Another nightmare for you would have been if one or two players had raised and/or reraised on the flop. Raises reduce your pot odds. Meanwhile, those players have hands while you have just a prayer, and you'll be facing more bets on the

The hard lessons here are these:

- Don't chase with borderline odds. Get a good overlay from the pot.

- If you are going to justify calls with pot odds, make sure you're going for the nuts.

- Be careful using pot odds to call with more than one card to come, unless you're going all-in.

- Realize that if someone raises, the pot odds might no longer be there to call.

turn. You don't want to be calling raises with just a draw. The pot odds rarely justify it, and you end up taking a big loss on a speculative hand. That's what you want *them* to do!

Other Applications for Pot Odds

You will encounter some real loose games, both at home and in the casino, if you start out playing lower-limit poker. In some games, almost the whole table will see fourth street in Stud or the flop in Hold'em. But you don't want to invest in trash starting hands that drain your chips. So what do you do? Pot odds can help here. Sure, you still want to be selective, and you don't want to just throw money in with everyone else and turn the game into an exercise in luck. But with so many players in there, it actually becomes correct to see a lot of flops in Hold'em and a lot of fourth streets in Stud.

In Stud, you could easily call with any three relatively high cards, any three to a straight, even any pair. In Hold'em, against six other players, you're obviously getting 6-1 odds preflop, so you can conceivably play any hand that has more than a 16-percent chance of winning. Those would include about any ace, K-7 and above, Q-9 and above, J-10 and above, and of course all the pairs and suited connectors. But don't just play any two suited cards, even though everyone else is.

POKER POINTER

When counting your "outs," ask yourself if someone could be holding one of your cards. Consider the board and the other player's betting pattern. If he does have one of your cards, that changes your odds and impacts your decision to call or fold—and might be the difference between winning and losing.

If you're new to the game, pot odds can also help you decide whether to call that final bet on the river. If you're playing well, you have the lead, and you're the one who's bet on the river. But now that someone's bet into you and you don't have much, you're stuck. You have to go over the hand, the betting, and how the cards fell, and meld it with your knowledge of the player. Does he bluff? Could he have missed his draw and now be betting because it's his only chance?

If your poker skills haven't solved your dilemma, use pot odds. If you're facing a $10 bet here, and the pot's just $30, that's only 3-to-1 odds. If all you can beat is a bluff, he'll have to be bluffing one out of four times for you to break even calling. With a pot this small, it's probably not worth it.

But say it's a $100 pot. That's 10-to-1. The size of the pot and the odds have your attention. If chances are greater than

9 percent that he's bluffing, you should call. If you catch someone trying to buy one just one out of eleven times, you break even. If you catch someone twice out of eleven times, you're up $110!

Be Wary of "Implied Odds"

"Implied odds" is a fancy way of saying that if you hit a big hand, you believe you'll get a big payoff, with some raising and reraising on the river. Many feel you can use these future bets—if you are sure they will occur—to justify a call even if the pot odds are below what they should be. The future rewards will be that great.

POKER POINTER

A lot of players use "implied odds" to justify calling with speculative drawing hands just because they want to stay in action, not because the future payoff justifies it. Don't fall into that trap.

For example, take this Hold'em scenario. You have K♥ and Q♠. After the turn the board is K♠, J♠, 2♠, Q♥. You feel that one opponent has a straight, the other an ace-high flush. The full house you hope to get will blow them away. You have four outs out of forty-six cards, or about 10-1 odds. It's a $5–$10 game. It's going to cost you $10 to see the river, and there's $70 in the pot. You're getting 7-1, but you need 10-1. You feel, however, that if you hit the nuts, you can get $20 out of each of them. With implied odds, you are getting $110 for that $10 call on the turn (11-to-1), if your "feeling" is correct.

Used correctly, pot odds can be a faithful ally, not a surreptitious enemy. But pot odds and implied odds can be misused if players are just looking for an excuse to stay in a hand. A good player, in general, is wary of chasing—despite the odds, he is still a longshot, and the payoff will occur over the long term, over many games. In the near term, chasing four-flushes and four-straights could put you in the hole.

CHAPTER 3

POKER PSYCHOLOGY

Poker is a game of deception. But it's not just the cards that must be hidden; you must also hide you. After all, the person throwing raises at you has plans and schemes, and his personality, his emotions—who he is—permeate every move he makes. But while you're figuring out what makes him tick, he's going to be staring right back at you.

Your Table Image

The way you are viewed while you battle for chips is called your table image. From the moment you sit down, you should mold your image to be the way *you* want it. You choose the image that will win you the most money in a particular game, and then develop it. If anyone catches on, just as with aggressive play, change gears. You do not have to play like your real personality. Each poker game is an opportunity for you to re-create yourself. The most important image considerations include the following.

- Be aware of the "vibe" you are projecting at the table.
- Manipulate that vibe for sound strategic purposes.
- Be aware of how opponents will react to that vibe.

If you know how others will respond, then, to an extent, you are controlling their play. You can use those responses to make your foes predictable—and then make good plays of your own. This is just another way to keep opponents crossed up and guessing.

What follows are some basic personality types many good players watch for when evaluating new blood. Closely observe the game you plan to join. You will have to decide when it is to your advantage to show your true colors when you sit down, and when it's better to represent an alter ego.

The Timid Type
The nonaggressive person gives himself away by not looking people in the eye, talking softly, being run out of pots, hesitating, not betting his good hands strongly, calling all the way down on losing hands, checking and calling too much, not raising enough, and not bluffing in obvious bluffing situations. With some shy types, this loose, passive play is replaced by play that is tight and passive, what is known as "weak-tight," where the person folds all but "sure thing" starting hands and rarely bets.

If You're Laid Back, Hide It
You don't want to be challenged by bluffers and players trying to run you over or buy pots at your expense. It's hard enough without constantly being put to a decision. So use

some phony bluster to hide that you are new and unsure or that your natural bent is to play tight and quietly wait for good hands. Bet it up early, take a few chances, slam some bets down, semi-bluff, and speak strongly and confidently. Know the game and the rules—don't ask questions. Learn to shuffle your chips like the pros. *Make your first impression the opposite of how you intend to play.* Most people never go beyond first impressions when sizing up a new player.

The Deception Factor

To your foes, timid equals scared, and scared means "tight." That's why you should hide your quiet nature with tough posturing if you need to hunker down, such as in a real loose game. While others are thinking you are just one of the gamblers, you take pots by playing better hands and folding more. Study those loud, loose players to pick up mannerisms you can employ when conservative is your strategy. And if tight is the only way you can play comfortably, it is all the more important to hide that fact.

However, you do not have to play tight just because you have a retiring nature. Find a conservative game, and go be the aggressor. And if you plan to be aggressive, it isn't a bad idea to have them peg you for being tight, so—lucky you— you can just be yourself for a while after you sit down.

The Bully Type

These aggressive players are dangerous, except the ones who overdo it and turn into ego-driven maniacs who play too loose, don't realize when to back off, and get themselves trapped by rocks with premium cards. Most players observing a boisterous personality think "loose," and loose usually means easy money.

If this is your personality, it will be hard to hide it, but if you are against quality opponents, you will do yourself a favor by acting tight and even a little timid at first. Then, when you start betting, your bets will be respected. You'll be able to rake a lot of pots that you would be called down on if others thought you were just a loud-mouthed yahoo full of hot air.

POKER POINTER

If you're a bully type, and you find you're called too often or are bluffing off too many chips, you must rein yourself in. Bullies can lose more chips in an hour than a drunken roulette player. It may not be your nature to be tight, but against top players you will have to try. Find a slower gear—your wallet will love you for it.

If you're heading for a game that's tight, you will want to play looser, so start out imitating the rocks. Fold a lot, and make sure they notice. Fold to others' bets, and talk about it. Even lie about what you folded—and have it be some sure-winning hand that even the rocks would have called with. Then when you bring out your "A" game and start taking over, the rocks won't think you're full of it. They'll give your raises respect—at least for a while.

If you're in a wild game, you will want to be tighter than the field, even if every particle of your being is crying out to reraise these maniacs. So go in ramming for a loose first impression, then tighten up without letting them realize it. Still talk your macho game here, just don't play it!

The Thinker

These players are always looking around, trying to pick up tells, and analyzing. These are positive traits, to be sure, but thinkers are way too obvious about it. Good players can do all these things without seeming to.

When a thinker is at the table, he is a target for false tells and manipulation. The sharks know he is watching. They have an audience, unlike most of the time, when they are not sure if an opponent is smart enough to be ensnared by a move. They know what the thinker is looking for, and they can use that. The good players will make "obvious bluffs" with good hands, and they'll deploy transparent tells the thinker is sure to see to trap him next time.

How to Hide That You're a Thinker

To keep others from playing with your head, use deception. Be more of a good ol' boy and less of a professor. Thinkers are expected to play only top starting hands, so take some chances early. Some thinkers can hold their own with good technical play, but computer wizards who think they can roll into town for a convention and play with the big boys are in for a rude awakening. If you are attending a convention, don't tell anyone—and don't look the part. This is one time you should dress down and act like the locals if you are serious about winning.

Acting Dumb

If you're not the smartest person in the world, first, ask yourself why you're playing for money. The fact is, there aren't many dim bulbs playing poker anywhere but in $2–$4 games and at the kitchen table. So acting dumb when you are smart, as some locals do, is an iffy proposition. They ask dumb questions, talk like yahoos, and appear to be just throwing chips around without thinking.

But the act is transparent. For one thing, after one or two good moves, it'll be obvious they know what they're doing. And the intensity can't be disguised. It is obvious they are playing to win—every hand. Acting stupid just doesn't work in poker. Intelligence has an energy to it that cannot be hidden.

Tourists and Top Players

Nothing makes the casino locals salivate like the sight of tourists. In fact, to the regulars, being called a "tourist" is a serious insult. Unless your game is killer, you don't want to be pegged as a tourist. Though it is not always true, regulars believe tourists are poor players. So they target the visitors in the game and try moves they wouldn't try on other locals who've seen it all before.

If you're really skilled, of course, you might just make a little cash acting like a tourist, but "dumbing down your look" while still playing skillfully is an acting job worthy of De Niro. You'd better have a lot of miles on you before you try that, because acting dumb makes you a target and is generally an unsound strategy.

Tourist Traps

Here are some "tourist" characteristics to avoid. First, don't look the part: no farmer hats from your hometown, outfits you would only wear on vacation, Hawaiian shirts, shorts, high socks, or T-shirts from your local auto parts store. Next, don't act the part. No fancy umbrella cocktails. Don't ask

"Where are you from?" or let your spouse come by to wish you good luck. At that point, you'll need it.

POKER POINTER

Many games will be comprised of players of all stripes—loose, tight, and "just right," and both aggressive and passive. But when people have played together for a long time (such as a tableful of locals), they tend to play very much alike.

If you are a new face, many opponents will automatically assume you are from out of town, and they will thus assume you play poorly. That arrogance is their weakness. Use it. Find the prevailing strategy at your table (usually some rock-like approach learned from some ancient book), and then start playing with their heads. Let them think you're loose or passive, and then disappoint them.

How Not to Tip People Off You're a Rookie

Avoid these dead giveaways if you don't want anyone to know you're new to the game: carrying chips from a lower-limit table to a higher-limit game, reading the rules posted on the wall, asking questions, betting (and acting) in a manner that is not smooth and clean, being too inconsistent in your actions, slow-playing too much, chattering too much, not understanding the blinds, acting unsure, not sticking up for yourself, not being ready for raises or being run at, being intimidated, being too tight or too loose, not being able to get away from a hand, thinking everyone's bluffing you, not being able to "shuffle" chips, or acting uncomfortable.

Facing Very Good Players

If you must try your hand against good opponents, they will likely be more tight than loose, so a tight demeanor might work better. Then your bets will get more respect. But you will quickly notice that these players are not too tight or too loose, but "just right." And they will be more experienced at discerning table image—real and fake—than you. They will also be betting their good hands aggressively. You will not know when they are bluffing. They will be very aware of how much is in the pot.

Acting like a tourist is probable suicide against these guys, but if you do, some may try to run you out or bluff, so you can pick up chips when you put the nuts on them. For the more sober-minded, acting like a pro with pros is wiser. It'll take some study to master that. You won't make much headway, but at least you won't be picked on.

Take caution: When you are against good players, they will be looking at the hands you show down as much as anything else to decide your style. So if you are showing down just top hands, they will think you are solid (a good player) or tight (a cautious rock). You can then play a little looser.

On the other hand, if you've been called trying to ram-and-jam a hand through and ended up losing, and you've had to turn up some questionable cards more than once, they will view you as loose, so you must now play tighter (only premium hands)—while still projecting a ram-and-jam personality. From then on, your loose image will get your top hands called.

The Four Classic Styles of Play

There are four distinct types of casino players, and your strategy against each will be markedly different. You will fall into one of these categories as well—more or less—but you will outplay your foes, first by changing your style of play during a game and adapting your style to the specific players you're facing; and second, by disguising which type you are at any given moment by playing "against" your personality, and by giving verbal and visual cues that identify you as a different

Since you will usually play against your image in order to sow the maximum confusion in the minds of the enemy, try these image plays:

- In a tight game, you will want to play looser, so create a tight image.
- In a loose game, you will want to play tighter, so use a loose image.
- If you are sitting with weak players, act like they do. Your skills will soon take over.
- If you are a "tourist," don't act like it unless you are really skilled.
- If you are a tourist playing with locals, your persona should depend on whether they are loose or tight.
- If you are a local playing with tourists, be friendly and don't act like you're just there to grind it out.

If you want to fit in and act like a low-limit local, dress drably, never smile, whisper when you talk, and act like you're working, not playing.

type than you really are. Of course, you'll be on the alert for other savvy players doing the same. The four types are discussed here, in order from weakest to strongest.

"Loose" and "tight" refer to how many hands a person plays and how long he or she stays in the hand. "Passive" and "aggressive" describe how strongly a person bets with a hand, and how often someone will bluff, semi-bluff, or push an advantage, even a small one.

The Loose-Passive Player

Loose-passive is the weakest way to play. Loose-passive types play too many hands, which means they are second-best (or worse) starting out. They stick with the hands too long, so they often just call all the way, where they are again second-best. They always believe someone is trying to bluff them, and a lot of people have gone broke trying to, because loose-passives will always call if they've stayed to the river. This is the type who will "keep you honest." Known as "calling stations," they come to play, and it pains them to fold a hand. In fact, they will keep calling if there is even the remotest chance of hitting a hand. They don't understand outs, odds, and pot odds.

This is the type that always seems to be putting a bad beat on you, but in reality, this is the player who is feeding you the most chips. Sure, he'll hit a longshot draw once in a while, but that's good, because he'll be less inclined to change his style. Whatever you do, don't criticize his play, and if he beats you, just say "Nice hand"—like you mean it! Calling stations are common in low-limit, and if you have a few loose-passives in a game, it will be hard for you to lose.

Loose-passives will play almost anything in almost any position. If they have 9-5 offsuit, it's, "Hey, I could make a straight!" Any two suited cards, and it's "Hey, I could make a flush." The problem with the "passive" part of their play is that when they finally get in the lead, they don't bet it. They're real liberal when it comes to contributing to the pot, but not when it comes to pushing a slight edge. They don't isolate, buy pots, and won't use their passive image to steal a blind. If they bet, you know they've got a real hand, so that's your cue to fold like your cards are on fire.

The Tight-Passive Player

Of all the player types, tight-passives are held in the most contempt. Also known as "weak-tight," they play like their last meal is on the line. These "rocks" will wait and wait for a good starting hand, but they rarely bet it when they get one.

Tight-passives have an idea of position but not of isolation. They will get angry when you raise their blinds—or raise at all—and if *they* raise, they expect you to fold. In Stud, they will raise the maximum on third street with an ace showing, but if you call, you'll get a dirty look. Their idea of odds is a sure thing—having a 2-to-1 edge isn't enough for a bet.

Tight-passives often check on the river with the best hand if they don't have the nuts, and they play as if they expect their opponent to have the best possible hand.

With such a tight image, a bluff from a tight-passive would be powerful, but they rarely try it—the money is just too precious. When these players bet, you can be sure they have something. If they raise, they've got the nuts! If a rock is in the hand past the flop, there's a reason—and it won't be a draw. These players can be driven from pots, but be careful. Many of them are stubborn. If one is in with his premium starting hand, he will very often call you down. Their feeling is that you should respect their tight image and give them the pot when they're in it. If you are going to bluff, make sure there's a scary flop and you have been betting your hand like you have what you are representing. Remember, they fear the worst, so bet like you have it.

The Loose-Aggressive Player

Loose-aggressives can single-handedly change the nature of an entire game. Unfortunately for them, and fortunately for you, their aggression is extreme—not controlled. They are not selective, and they don't back off soon enough when they encounter strength.

These loose players are the serial daters of poker; they've never met a hand they didn't fall in love with. Called "mani-acs," they can drive good players crazy, because good players won't call even a crazy man with just anything. And their aggressiveness takes away many of the good players' moves. Like the loose-passives, they play too many hands, and they see a lot of flops in Hold'em and fourth and fifth streets in

Stud. But unlike the elephants, maniacs will bet their hands. And bet them big. It seems like they are always bluffing and "betting on the come." Even when you realize they are pushing some hands that aren't all that good, you will have to risk some serious money to beat them.

ASK JOHNNY QUADS

Do cardrooms use shills and proposition players to start games?

Yes. *Shills* play with casino money and are called on to start new tables or keep games going when players are scarce. *Props* are good players paid an hourly wage by a cardroom to fill empty seats on demand. Props use their own money and keep their winnings. Shills are tight-passive; props are more aggressive.

If the maniacs are catching cards, they can win a bundle. They control the game, and they sure know how to build a pot. But sooner or later, they have to pay the piper. You can only go in with second-best hands so often before folks get the stones to call you down. You can lose a lot of chips in a great big hurry trying to ram through speculative hands, like four-flushes, four-straights, and Q-9 suited. When they start getting beat, they go on tilt.

The Tight-Aggressive Player

Compared to the other three types, tight-aggressive players are experts. They are selective about their starting hands and will vary those hands according to position. They play fewer hands than the maniacs and calling stations, but more than the rocks. But the big difference between experts and rocks is that when experts enter a hand, they go in betting or raising. Expert players protect their hands, bet them, and push the lead—however slight—and they know when to back off.

POKER POINTER

It isn't just the players who will fit (more or less) into categories—the games themselves will also. You can think of the game you're in as loose-passive, loose-aggressive, tight-passive, or tight-aggressive. You make this judgment mainly by the amount of betting and raising that's going on, the quality of the hands being played, and how many see the flop.

Unlike the calling stations and maniacs, experts don't just play their own hands. Their strategy is based on what they think their opponents have. They are aggressive, but unlike the loose-aggressives, they are selective. Experts aren't relentlessly driving at pots, so their bets maintain respect.

What Does It Mean When They Bet?

When a calling station or a rock bets, be very afraid. The calling station has the nuts (or what he thinks is the nuts), and the rock has one of the premium hands he waits all day for. If the maniac bets—well, he always bets, doesn't he? When he doesn't bet—that's when you need to worry. Either he's taking a hand off to catch his breath, or he might actually have a real hand this time. If the expert bets, he probably has something, but more likely he's just betting because you didn't.

There's a strategy point regarding experts, especially those who have dropped down from higher limits. When you evaluate this person, remember that he is used to folding a lot of hands after a bet, because the high-limit games are tighter. So he will be susceptible to a bluff. He's used to laying a hand down—the exception being the high-limit player who is playing too loose after he drops down due to the smaller stakes. In this case, he will surely lose.

POKER POINTER

A raise from a rock or calling station should mean an immediate fold, and while one from an expert is to be feared, be alert for position bets and bluffs, especially if others appear weak. A bet from a maniac usually means nothing—he will only rarely hit his hand.

And here's an interesting dilemma when it comes to maniacs. If you are in a short-handed game, he will be tough to beat, as his wide-open play is tailor-made for four players or fewer, when you must play more (and weaker) hands and take some chances to keep the blinds and antes from killing you. If you are short-handed with this type, your best course is to find another table. He will either force you to toss some winning hands or call him all the way to the river with your unpaired ace, hoping for the best.

CHAPTER 4

GET YOUR
HOME GAME ON

An introduction to poker through "home games" with friends, family, and acquaintances is truly a blessing. These will be some of the most enjoyable games of your life, short of winning thousands on the World Poker Tour. There is no place better than home to discover the joy of poker.

Setting House Rules

Since you're on the honor system, you have to play with people you trust, and you must shun those who violate that trust. It is poker, so you are trying to win money—that is part of the fun. But that is not all of it. Camaraderie is important, too. Without the casino floor people to settle disputes, you're on your own, so you need to have the rules and etiquette straight.

Before the game begins, decide who is the bank, what time the game ends, if anyone must leave early, if "check-raising"

(raising after having previously checked) is allowed, what constitutes a misdeal and how it will be handled, what the stakes will be, and how many raises are allowed. Also decide if you will play "table stakes," where players only risk the chips in front of them, or if they will be allowed to bet and call bets with cash pulled out of their pockets.

The Typical Home Game

You will be amazed at how similar home games are all over the world. They're friendly, affordable gatherings with maybe one guy playing over his head, and one or two under theirs. There are really only two variations: first are the games that are real loose, with a lot of people just calling, and second are the games that are real loose, with a lot of people raising.

The first variation is definitely more plentiful. The common denominator is that there are a lot of people in every hand, even on the later streets, and tight players are thought strange. Folks have come to play, so they play a lot of starting hands—and stick with them. They want to be in action, not on the sidelines. Hunches are followed, not the odds. A miracle draw is reason enough to call a bet or even a raise. Bluffing isn't easy, and often players call with next to nothing just to "keep you honest."

In the best of the games, there will be drinking, smoking, eating, loose talk, and a lot of banter. Groups have been known to meet regularly for a decade or more.

The Way to Win

While it's true that "luck" is a bigger factor in home games than in a casino, it's still the skillful players who win over time. You just have to adapt. You can still play solid poker, but you won't be as tight as in a casino. First of all, if you're too tight, you'll get abuse from your buds. Second, with more players in the hand and bigger pots, you will have the odds to play some marginal hands that won't hit as often but that will pay off big when they do.

Fold More Often Than Your Opponents

Even though you can play more starting hands, you're still going to fold more hands than most of the others, and you're not going to stay with the hand if it doesn't develop fast (unlike your pals). Even though others may be in with some real trash, with so many hands out there you're not guaranteed a win. *Money saved is money earned.* You *can* be patient at home—just try to play tight without appearing to. Complain about your bad hands when you fold. They'll understand.

POKER POINTER

Even pocket aces, the best starting hand in Hold'em, are an underdog in a large field. Aces win **88** percent of the time against one player, but against six random hands staying to the river, they're lucky to win half the time.

Starting out with second-best hands is asking to be second-best at the river, and this is how you lose the most money. Watch your home game, and you'll see for yourself: The loosest player at the table may win a lot of pots, but he'll be the big loser most often, because he's always finishing second. Better to drop out of the race than to be runner-up.

When You Have It, Bet It

Don't worry about people folding when you have a monster hand, unless it's sitting on the board. No one's going to believe you have it. These folks came to play. They didn't come to fold. Your winning hand will get paid off, even on the river. You don't have to finesse people with check-raises. Just bet. In fact, check-raises might just *lose* you money, because that's one of the few times they'll believe you have the nuts.

Bluff Early

They say you can't bluff in a loose game, but unless the stakes are too low, you *can* do it selectively. Know your players. There always will be someone to bluff, either a player over his head financially, one afraid of losing, or one who analyzes too much. But there will be many more who would rather throw in that last bet than risk being bluffed out. And you can't bluff someone who isn't skilled enough to know what your bets mean and put you on a hand. In large pots, as in many casino games, someone will "sheriff" the pot when it gets huge. Someone will "keep you honest."

But getting caught bluffing isn't all bad in a home game. In fact, it is a good idea to bluff early and often, *until you are caught*. Make sure when you are nabbed that everyone knows it. The memory of this bluff will stick with them all night, and for many games to come, so stop trying to buy pots for awhile. Meanwhile, your opponents will pay off your big hands over and over again with nothing.

Read Your Fellow Players

Some pros say that reading players is futile in a wild home game, but that couldn't be further from the truth. Home players are actually easier to read because they are less skilled and less guarded. Some are advanced enough to at least try to mask their feelings, but they never get beyond the "acting weak when strong, strong when weak" stage. You won't have to look too deep to figure a player out.

How to Spot a Bluff

The few who bluff will act noticeably different during their bluff. The talker will suddenly be still, the quiet one will talk, the nervous one will be calm, and the calm one nervous. Bluffing is so rare it's easy to spot. It's also easy to tell if someone's on a draw or just how strong his hand is. Players' bets are not consistent. The mannerisms and force vary. They are open books, and you can use this information to win at home.

Is He Bluffing or Just Drunk?

Drinking and poker don't mix, unless your primary objective is to drink with poker as a little diversion. If you must drink, only do it at a home game, and at least be less impaired than your buds. Raking in pots is just as much fun as blindly throwing money around in a drunken stupor.

Watch for changes in style as players drink. Just when you didn't think the game could get looser, it does. Some players who never bet and never bluff might actually do both. Players will try to drive you out of pots, or refuse to fold, and you may take some bad beats from players who don't even know what hand they have. Just chalk it up to the charm of a home game!

POKER POINTER

Watch out for false tells with drunken players, and tells that have changed from when they were sober. Also, it can be very hard to read a player too drunk to know—or care!—what he has.

Go Crazy!

Part of the appeal of a home game is that the dealer can call any game he wants. Crazy community-card games like Criss-Cross, games where you pass cards to other players, games with one or more wild cards . . . it's enough to make a serious player throw up. But not so fast! Before you look down your nose at these games, think about what a gold mine they really are. Wild games build pots. And the pots are built by wishful thinking a good player can exploit.

If you are a student of poker and one of the better players at the table, you should easily be able to make money with these variations. It's quite simple. Most players don't understand that you need a monster hand to win wild-card games, and they wind up pursuing straights and flushes when someone always has a full house, or a full house in games where you know someone will get at least four of a kind. And no matter what the game, you can still calculate your outs.

Common Mistakes

To win home games, just avoid the following bad plays your opponents will frequently make.

- Slow-playing strong hands. Giving free cards so other players will stay in and build a pot will get you beat.
- Not raising enough. Raise when you're ahead. Don't wait for a lock. And make sure you raise on the river.
- Being afraid to fold. You're not less of a man—or woman—if you fold. Play smarter than them.
- Not realizing that with more players in, it will usually take a better hand than usual at the river to win.
- Not having fun, win or lose. Be a good sport so you'll be invited back. Don't be a sore loser or a sore winner!
- Not knowing who the dangerous player in your home game is. He's the one to watch.

Remember these few pieces of advice, and your home game will always be fun and profitable.

CHAPTER 5

TIME TO HIT
THE CASINO

Home games are fun, but every good poker player eventually yearns for the adrenaline rush of a casino game. At a casino, you choose the game, the table, and the stakes. You leave whenever you want, and you'll always get your winnings. But there are some big differences between casino poker and your home game. Read on and learn how to recognize a good game when you graduate from the kitchen table to the bright lights and glitz of the gambling hall.

A Whole New Game
While a home game is a wonderful chance to learn and have fun, you have to unlearn a few things when you hit the casino, where you will usually be competing against better players. You can't expect to make as much money from the mistakes of others—you're going to have to earn it. It will be

much more difficult to be dominant. Among your friends, you can play a little looser and use your (hopefully) greater knowledge of the game to take over, but that's much harder to do among strangers.

Patience to the Fore!

At home you can play more hands. Not only is it expected, but with everyone else in, the pots are big enough for you take some chances. In most casino games, folks play tighter. You're going to be facing strong hands, so you must have a hand yourself. That means waiting for good cards. Patiently.

ASK JOHNNY QUADS

What is "limping in"?

"Limping in" means entering the hand by calling someone else's bet, rather than by raising. Limping is a questionable play because though you've thrown money in the pot, you've shown weakness in doing so. Someone will bet at you on the next round.

A Raise Means What It Says

Unlike at home, where a raise could mean anything, in the casino a raise usually means what it says: I've got a hand. There are players who will bluff, sure, but they pick their spots. You need to quickly get a line on the players who will and won't, but for the most part, unless someone's targeting you as a "new guy" and trying to run you over, a raise means what it says. That goes double for reraises and triple for check-raises. You might go years without seeing a check-raise bluff in a lower-limit game, so don't assume everyone's trying to bluff you. A raise is sending you a message—figure out what it is.

Yes, a raise means you're facing a good hand in the casino, but the higher the limit, the more you will face bluffs and semi-bluffs (bluffing with outs). The difference from your home game is that casino bluffers know *when* to bluff. They will bluff when they know you have nothing—and often win—even when their "nothing" is worse than yours.

In addition to the raises having more behind them, you'll face more strategic raises. Good players would rather cut off a toe than let you just limp in and see cards cheaply. If you're on a draw, you'll have to pay for it. If you haven't taken control of a hand by showing some power, someone else will.

Reading Players: Home Versus Casino

Even the sober home players have unguarded moments and transparent tricks. The tricky homies will act the opposite of what they have, but there's nothing more obvious than someone who acts all sad and then suddenly raises you! Players love to talk at home, and the more they talk, the more they give away. These giveaways—the loose talk laden with clues, the failure to vary their play—are money in your pocket.

POKER POINTER

Don't be a "calling station"—a timid player who keeps calling bets, but never takes control by raising. Such a player is seen as weak. He rarely wins because he needs to hit his hand to take the pot. Bettors can win by sheer force. Callers cannot.

If you are playing any kind of reasonable limit, you will rarely find these mistakes in the casino, where players are making a conscious effort not to give anything away. The clues to their holdings are much more subtle. You won't hear a lot of talk or see players ready to fold before their turn. The good ones have gone beyond the poker face. They have poker bodies. When there is movement, they strive to make it controlled and consistent. Your opponents will have seen it all before and will be watching you.

Your First Casino Game

You will have an easier time if you are not pegged as a rookie right off the bat. Learn as much as you can about the protocols before you hit the cardroom, so you can act like you belong. If you act like a pro, people just might think you are one.

Step Up to the Plate

Whether you start in a California cardroom with hundreds of tables or a small casino with just a few, walk in like you own the place. There will be a sign-up board on the wall listing all the games, or a sign-up sheet at a desk. (Sometimes the sign-up for higher limits is in a different area than lower limit.) Don't wait for a floorperson to ask you what you want. Walk right up to him and tell him which game you want and the limit, and he'll take you to your table or put you on the waiting list.

If there's a wait, ask where the tables are with your limit, so you can start observing play. This will put you way ahead of the game when you do sit down to play. Watch who's controlling the action, whether it's tight or loose, and start looking for tells, which are often easier to spot when you're

In a casino, even two or three weak players can make a game profitable, but more often than not you'll be facing players who know the game as well as (or better than) you do. Here are some things to watch for:

- Casino players will test you. They'll invest chips to feel you out.

- You will be facing better hands. Players don't toss in chips to be "in action." You'll have fewer callers.

- In the casino, folks will call you with a draw (for example, a four-flush) if the pot is large. At home, they'll always call you.

- If you don't bet, someone else will. Someone will try to run you out if you show any weakness.

- The higher the stakes, the better the players, though some weak players can be found at every level.

- You can't give "free" cards. "Luring people in" with a big hand is a recipe for disaster. Take the sure thing.

- Home players are always looking for the big score. Good casino players just want a score.

- You won't find many drinkers at the table. Good players know better and seek out drunks to beat them, not join them.

Don't be daunted by casino players or think they are all experts just because they talk a good game. They have their tells and weaknesses, otherwise they'd be playing $300–$600 limit in Vegas.

away from the table. The floorperson will page you when a seat is available. If you're not near him, raise your hand—quickly—so he can see it, or he'll give the spot to someone else. The floorperson may ask how many chips you want, or you may have to get them from the dealer.

Read the Rules

At home, you establish house rules. In the casino, the basics will be posted. Read them, without drawing attention to the fact you're doing it, which would tip everyone off that you are new. The rules will cover such things as limits, number of raises, buy-ins, the rake, profanity, and the like. If you still have questions, quietly ask a floorperson or dealer on break.

POKER POINTER

Casinos play "cards speak." At the showdown, just turn over your hand and let the dealer call what you have. But make sure he is right about your hand and your opponent's! You'd be surprised at how often they are wrong. And turn over all your cards.

All casinos play table stakes—you cannot bet (or lose) more than you have on the table. When you put your last chip in the pot, announce that you are "all-in." All casinos allow check-raising.

Casinos don't allow "string bets," that is, putting some chips in the pot, then reaching back to your stack to get more to raise. If you do this, you will not be allowed to bump it up. To avoid this faux pas, simply have enough chips in your hand to cover your raise, or, much better yet, just announce "Raise."

Poker-Table Protocol

You can get away with a lot at home, but this is not true in a casino, where your cards must stay on the table. You can't look at anyone's else's hand, you can't comment on the hand if you've folded, and in many rooms you can't even discuss your own hand. You also can't stash cash in your pocket if you've sold someone chips, which should only be done after checking with the dealer.

Follow the common-sense etiquette from your home game: Act in turn, be ready to act when it's on you, don't slow down the game, don't splash the pot, don't abuse other players or the dealer, and be a good sport. Try not to whine, complain, or criticize someone who has beaten you out of a pot. And you don't have to say anything when you win a pot. Just rake in the chips.

Choosing a Seat

Ask for a chair that is at one end of the table, not across from the dealer. From the end, you can see the entire table in front of you. It's easy to watch the action and spot tells. Across from the dealer, you can't see anything but the dealer's mug, and you're constantly swiveling your noggin around. You end up seeing the side of a lot of heads. If you get stuck in one of these seats, tell the dealer you want to change seats when someone leaves. If a new dealer comes in, tell him too. And always be on the lookout for a more profitable table. Just quietly tell the floorperson you want a table change.

POKER POINTER

The seats at a poker table are numbered, starting to the dealer's left and going clockwise, ending with the seat on his right. There are ten seats at a Hold'em table, eight for Stud. The most advantageous seats are 2, 3, 8, and 9 for Hold'em, and 2, 3, 6, and 7 for Stud.

Tipping

Yes, tip the dealer. Most casinos used to have quarters and fifty-cent pieces in the game for tips, but that is becoming rare. Today, with the $1 chip usually the lowest denomination, you will tip a buck. Remember, to you, the "toke" is just another rake—it's more money out of play. But don't take it out on the dealer: It isn't easy making a living a dollar at a time. And you definitely want him or her on your side. It's bad business to alienate the person running the game and handling the cards. Give the dealer his due.

ASK JOHNNY QUADS

What is "under the gun"?

The person under the gun is to the left of the big blind and is first to act during the first betting round in Hold'em. He must call the big blind's "bet," raise, or fold. In future rounds, the big and small blinds act before him if they have not folded.

Playing in a Loose Game

As much as anything else, it's whether the game is loose, tight, or in between that will determine your play. You should know the type of game you'll be embroiled in before you even sit down so you can adopt the correct strategy from the very first hand. So watch first, and then sit.

What Is a Loose Game?

Loose games are easy to spot. They are more animated, with much raising and reraising before the flop and frequent capped pots. When there's not a lot of raising, many players are limping in. Whether it's a "raise-fest" or not, the common denominator in loose games is a lot of players seeing the flop—and big pots. You'll notice a "snowball effect" in many loose games. The player "under the gun" limps in, perhaps with 10-9, a marginal early position hand. Had he raised, this would have made it two bets to go from early position, and many might have folded their borderline hands, fearing still another raise. But since he limped, the next guy decides this might be a big pot building, so he limps in too, also with a questionable early position hand like K-10. Others limp as well, dreaming of a big pot. The pot is now to the point where two things happen. First, no one in late position is going to fold preflop—with so many players, it is correct to limp in with almost any two hole cards. Second, no one expects anyone in late position to raise, as no one will fold for one more bet due to the pot size. Even pocket aces in Hold'em are an underdog to a huge field, and A-K is an underdog (41 percent) to just four players. This is the perfect scenario for those looking to "get lucky." And even in the raise-fest loose game, raises won't always drive players out. Sometimes they will "drive them in"!

Strategy in Loose Games

Many good players avoid loose games. But if you can handle the bankroll swings, these games can be quite lucrative. There's always a ton of chips up for grabs, and because so many players play marginal starting hands, they overrate their hole cards and don't fold soon enough on later streets. They get in the habit of playing bad hands and draws, and most continue their questionable play even after the game tightens up, as it inevitably will.

Realize you are going to have some money fluctuation in a loose game. You are not going to be as loose as the others—not even close—but you are going to be looser than usual. You *are* going to limp in for one bet with many more starting hands. You *are* going to chase open-ended straight and flush draws, even if there are raises, and you'll be playing second pairs (that is, the second highest pair possible on the board, not only the top pair). As with a loose home game, you still will be one of the tighter players—you just have to play solid without others finding out how tight you really are.

Some of your strategy is similar to a loose home game, so make sure you advertise how you're staying in pots. When you bet, act as wild as they do. Even in loose games, most players are very aware of who's tight. If you sit waiting for a monster hand, you probably won't get paid off.

The battlefield is littered with solid players who think they can jam it with A-K offsuit or pocket queens or jacks in a loose game. Other players just laugh and gladly toss in their money and build a pot. A-K is an underdog to a large field, and many a good player has left muttering "I can't play in this game" after his A-K has drained his chips and his opponent, while raking the pot, has laughed and said, "Ace-king no good!" If you are tighter than most of the field and are getting nowhere, and/or you're tired of battling the six or more players who see every flop, realize that you're probably playing stakes that are too low. Stay patient, or look for a more profitable game.

Recognizing a Tight Game

Tight games are as easy to spot as loose contests. Here are some dead giveaways:

- Players are generally older, and there isn't a lot of talking or smiling.
- Players look serious and want to get on to the next hand.
- Players spend a lot of time making sure their chips are in neat stacks.
- Reraising and check-raising are almost nonexistent.
- Few players see the flop. Fewer see the turn.
- Often, everyone folds to the blinds, who then "chop."

If you see a tight game, besides asking yourself if you're going to have any fun there, ask yourself if you have the time and patience needed to pry chips loose from these cheapskates. Your goal is to make money, and there's always another game right around the corner.

Strategy in a Tight Game

A winning strategy in a tight game is the opposite of a loose-game strategy. While you sometimes have to hunker down in a loose game, in a tight game you can be the aggressive one. With so many players just waiting for huge starting hands, you can raise and reraise with marginal hands and drive people out. Blind-stealing is easy, and an early raise will often get you heads-up. Realize if you're called that your tight opponent might have better cards than you, but you have a stronger weapon than cards—you have control of the hand,

and you're facing someone whose first instinct is to fold, not take chances. If the flop in Hold'em shows lower cards or fourth street in Stud gives him a blank (useless card), you bet it up and drive him out. If the flop or fourth street is stronger, you usually should bet even if you haven't improved. If your opponent beats you in the pot or raises(!), you simply fold. If someone shows you strength, drop out. Don't be stubborn if a rock finally gets the big hand he's been praying for. Just fold.

POKER POINTER

"Chopping" a pot means to split it, as in the case of a tie. The blinds can chop when everyone else has folded preflop. If both agree, they simply take their blinds back and the hand is over. Smart players chop because the House gets no rake. They avoid a hand in bad position and avoid paying a blind. If someone asks, "Do you chop?" say "Yes!"

If they catch on that you're buying pots, watch out for a bluff. Generally, though, it is against the nature of supertight players to risk their chips trying to buy one, especially against someone who shows strength. After awhile, your aggressive style will have the fringe benefit of getting your good hands paid off. Look for the threshold when they begin to catch on. They'll start calling you more often. Switch gears at that point, playing only quality hands that will take their chips "legitimately."

The Ideal Game
The best games, of course, are those where you're the best player at the table. The worst game is where everyone is better

than you. You can, however, do all right if there are *a few* better players, as long as you can quickly identify who they are. Most games have a few loose players, a few tight, and the rest in between: tight but not ridiculous, aggressive when need be, loose when appropriate. This pretty much should characterize your own play. If the majority are quality players, ask yourself if you can make money in the game. Often, even with good players at the table, a few weak players will be enough to give you a profit if you play smart.

ASK JOHNNY QUADS

How do I choose a game to play at the casino?

When you're new, steer clear of Omaha, and its cousin, Omaha 8 or Better. Omaha is an action game, and to win you're going to have to bet some well-calculated draws—and hit them. If you're comfortable with Seven-Card Stud (called simply "Stud" in the casino), this is a good game to start with. Hold'em, a fast game, is also great for the casino.

Avoid "Mucking" Mistakes

Here's a valuable tip: Unless everyone else has folded, just turn your cards face up and let the dealer read them and call your hand. Even if someone has flipped over a better hand, do it anyway. Someone may have miscalled his holding, or you could have misread your hand or your opponent's. If you throw your cards into the muck pile, or never turn them face up, your hand is disqualified and you cannot win. A hand turned face-up must be read by the dealer.

And if you have won the hand, whether against other players or because everyone else folded, do not throw away your cards (called mucking) *until the dealer pushes the pot to you.* Too many bad things can happen when you start flinging cards around. Even in cases where you do not have to show your hand (such as when everyone else has folded), don't do anything with your cards until the pot is actually passed to you. By the way, if you show your hand to one person, any other player can ask to see it as well.

Beware of someone calling out that he has a "full house" or "flush," and so on, especially before he's turned the cards over. An unethical player sometimes will call out a huge hand he doesn't really have, hoping his opponent will impulsively throw away (muck) his cards, making his hand dead. In that case, the original player wins the pot automatically.

Protect your hand. Keep chips or some heavy "lucky charm" on top of your hole cards to keep the dealer from mistakenly grabbing them and to keep others' mucked hands from accidentally hitting them. If those other cards touch yours, your hand is dead.

Keep an Eye on the Rake

Poker is one of the few games in a casino where you are not playing against the House. But the House has to be paid. It's running the game, giving you drinks, giving you space, buying equipment, paying employees, and, most importantly, ensuring you'll be paid when you win and not mugged when you leave the table, even if you quit while you're way ahead!

The payment to the House is called the *rake.* To a casino, the dealer's most important job is to remove chips from the pot and put them in the drop box. Standard rake is 5 or 10 percent up to a certain amount, such as $3, $4, or even $5 per hand. Don't ever play anyplace where there is no cap on the rake. As a rule, $3 is fair, $4 is borderline, and $5 or more is too high to beat, depending on the size of the average pot.

As a player, you want the rake to be as low as possible. The rake is your enemy. A rake that is too high—more than 5 percent of the pot, for example—will sap the stacks of everyone at the table and keep you from winning. Just as there are casino games, like roulette, where the House edge is just too high (5.26 percent) for you to ever show a long-term profit, so it is with an exorbitant rake.

ASK JOHNNY QUADS

Does the rake really matter?

Yes! Keep in mind that if there is a $3 rake, and the dealer is tipped a buck a hand, and you play thirty hands per hour, that's $120 taken out of play every sixty minutes! That's money that you will never see again. If eight players each started with $100, in less than seven hours the House would have every penny.

Seek out a low percentage relative to the typical pot. If the rake is $3, but the average pot is just $30, you're paying 10 percent! No one can win that way. If the pot is $60, and you're paying $3, that's 5 percent, the most you should pay but still a little high. If the average pot is $120 and you're paying $3, that's just 2.5 percent. Now you're talking! That is a beatable rake. You want high pots and a low rake, not the other way around!

POKER POINTER

The all-or-nothing nature of no-limit and pot-limit favor those who like insane—rather than calculated—risk. These games take years of experience to play well, and the learning curve can be an expensive one. Save these stakes for tournament play (if you absolutely must play them), where at least your loss is limited to the entry fee and the playing field is more level.

The advantage of casino poker is that if you are in an unprofitable game or you are surrounded by jerks, you can change tables. And if you are in a casino where the House is raking too much money, go find a cardroom in a different House.

What Stakes Should You Play?

Choosing the right stakes can be the difference between being happy or homeless after your poker experience. Today, everyone is mesmerized by no-limit poker, but the essential question you must ask yourself about no-limit (and pot-limit) poker is this: Why would you want to play in a game where you can lose every cent because of one bad beat, one unlucky card, or one clever play? No-limit and pot-limit—which are grouped together because you can easily have your whole stake in the pot on any given hand—give a huge advantage to the big-money boys with nothing to lose, no fear, and big expense accounts.

What stakes should you play? Pros say to play the highest you can comfortably afford, but on any given night you should pick the game where you have the greatest chance of winning, regardless of stakes.

Give yourself this test: If you have not called a bet because of the stakes, you are playing too high. If you have called a bet solely because it was "just a few bucks," you are playing too low. You'll feel it in your gut when you are "just right." Your ideal opponents are those who are nervous and intimidated by the stakes. Go find them!

CHAPTER 6

PLACE YOUR BETS

The language of poker isn't spoken with your lips; it's spoken with your chips. How and when you put your money in the pot says volumes about you and your hand, and these actions are a key to maximizing your profits. Betting is one of the supreme skills—and art forms—in the game. Bets send a message. It's imperative that the message that comes through is the one you want opponents to hear.

The Safety Zone
Your mathematical and psychological skills, along with your knowledge of the game, are all put in action through betting. Your bet forces your opponents to a decision. Do they want to put their hard-earned cash in there, or not?

Poker is all about psychology, guts, and most of all money—and having the courage to risk it. Risk is the key word. It can't be stressed enough: You have to be competing for something of real value, some significant amount of cold, hard cash, or there is no reason for anyone to ever fold a hand. If no one folds, you don't have a poker game—you just have a bunch of people sitting around waiting to see who's going to get lucky.

Play Stakes Where Their Hearts Are Racing

If you are just starting out in poker, *don't* play ultra-low-limit games like $1–$5, $1–$2, and $2–$4. You learn nothing in these loose games where people have nothing to lose; in fact, you'll pick up some bad habits, like just throwing chips in on a prayer. A borderline limit would be $4–$8, maybe okay until you get your feet wet, but graduate to $5–$10 or $6–$12 quickly, then $8–$16 and $10–$20. Keep moving up as long as you're winning.

POKER POINTER

To use poker skills, your bets must have some bite. They must put your opponents to the test. Make them think. Give them a chance to make a mistake. Therefore, you cannot use your skills in a game where the stakes are so low that calling a bet is meaningless.

Low-limit games can seem tempting, with so much poor play, but most good players hate them because they can't effectively use their skills: aggression, betting strategies, and reading players. If you are to bring your skills to bear through betting, your bets must put people to a decision, make them choke up, make them think—and fold. If the limits are too low, everyone will be in their safety zone, so none of that will happen.

The Easiest Money

Outside the zone means "scared money" in poker, and playing with scared money is the quickest way to lose. Playing against scared money is a piece of cake—just be aggressive. Every bet is a big decision to scared money, and it's written all over their faces. Scared players go into a shell and fold hand after hand they could've won, and only come out with a monster hand, at which point you will fold.

This is an extreme case. For your bets to be effective, you only need to be sure players seriously care about the chips in front of them. They must be concerned about losing them and be at the higher end of their comfortable limit, which is where many people play. It's easy to spot. Those who agonize and worry too much are out of their safety zone, while those who call bets too fast and too often and don't seem too concerned about much of anything are too far within theirs. Find a game where they're nervous—no matter what the stakes—and take over.

Making a Statement

A bet is first and foremost a declaration: *I have a better hand than you.* If no one ever tried to bluff a pot, most hands might end right there. Everyone would fold to the better hand. The conflict occurs when someone believes the bettor's full of hot air or thinks he has a better hand—or will have by the river. Anyone who disagrees with your declaration can argue the point by raising you, and if you think he's wrong, you can tell him so by reraising. If he's still not convinced, he can raise you back. It boils down to *convincing* the other guy you have the superior hand. If you ever watch two good heads-up players go at it, you'll see this reraising frequently—often when *they both have trash hands*—because it's become about who will blink first, not the cards.

Dominance on the Green Felt

The primary purpose of a bet is to establish dominance in the hand. Once control is established, the bettor will often win the pot without a fight—and without the good hand his bet claimed he had. Later, with skill and some good cards, that dominance can spread to the game as a whole. In most games, to attain a dominant position you'll need to bet up and show down some good hands at first. This gets folks used to thinking your bets have something behind them. It is a tremendous psychological advantage to be dominant in a game, as it is in life. But just as in life, you have to watch for the cunning types trying to trap you and bring you down.

POKER POINTER

Don't keep betting to establish dominance if it's obvious your opponent isn't going to drop and has a better hand than you. Back off and save your money. Plowing money into a lost cause will just make you look foolish and hurt you on future hands.

Bet with the Lead

To maintain dominance, you want to be betting it up, making other players think. But they've got to "respect" your raises. They can't just laugh at them or all pile in because they think you're a clown who's just thrown dead money in the pot. Your opponents must believe there's power behind your play. So when you've got the best hand—at any point—you bet it up big and keep the pressure on. This goes for before the flop in Hold'em relentlessly to the river, from third street in Stud to the last wager. You bet your hand strong—don't mess around. Betting is how you take over, so you seek every opportunity to bet it up.

When you're the favorite to win the hand, you bet to win the pot *right now*. Your lead is often more tenuous than you know, so you are satisfied to win whatever's there. Every hand begins as a struggle for the antes and blinds, and you're happy with those and any other sure thing this table will give you.

ASK JOHNNY QUADS

What's the best way to bet?

To avoid giving yourself away, the best way to bet is in a smooth, controlled, consistent manner, not too fast or too slow, the same way every time. Getting cute with different betting styles usually backfires. Focus your eyes on one thing. Don't look all over the place.

Most times, of course, you'll have callers. Then betting is your way to either drive people out or maximize your profit—or both. If you have top pair and top kicker on the flop, and everyone else just has overcards or draws, you're favored to win unless you're facing a huge field. So you bet and take their money, whether they stay or drop. If it's a big field, you still bet, this time to push people out.

Bet Like You Mean It

A bet indicates strength. So when you bet, bet strongly and forcefully. You don't have to slam your chips down, but you are stating you have a hand, so act like it. Putting chips in meekly either means you're playing your first game and are unsure of yourself (not something you want anyone to think), or you are pretending to be weak when you are strong, another rookie move. If you are weak, why are you betting?

ASK JOHNNY QUADS

What are "rolled-up" cards?

In Seven-Stud, if your first three cards are three of a kind, you are said to be "rolled-up." If you have three aces, for example, you are said to have "rolled-up aces." This is obviously an incredible hand.

A bet means a hand, so be confident. Then, when you are betting with nothing, you can bet the same way, and you have conditioned others to recognize that that betting style indicates a good hand, and they will be more likely to fold. This makes a lot more sense. Maybe you're one of those who want to keep people in a hand to build a pot. Well, first of all, you shouldn't be playing casino poker thinking like that—in a casino, you want to drive people out and grab the sure thing. Second, don't worry, because there's usually at least one rube who doesn't believe you and will call, at least for a street or two.

It's important to keep this in mind: Unless you have an unbeatable hand, you *want* people to think you have a top hand when you bet. You *want* them to fold. If your raises aren't respected, you may get some hands paid off, but you won't be able to bluff. You'll also be facing a larger field than you want—a field that will run you down hand after hand.

When Not to Bet

There are a few situations when you should not bet a big hand. One is when you are so far in the lead that if you bet, everyone will fold. For example, you flop a full house in Hold'em, and you've got all the cards. If the flop's K-K-Q, and you have K-Q, what can anyone else have? So check, and let them catch up a bit. Hope someone will bet into you, catch a second-best hand, or bluff at the pot!

Or if you have rolled-up high trips in a tight Stud game, you may want to play it coy. Same with flopping top set (where a board card has matched your pocket pair) in Hold'em against a small field if the board's not scary. But be wary. Except for when you have the mortal nuts, you will rarely go wrong betting, but you can go horribly wrong giving free cards to drawing hands.

Either Raise or Fold, But Rarely Call

A lot of good things happen when you bet, and a few things can happen when you don't—most of them bad. That's why as the limits get higher and the poker becomes more skilled, you'll realize that your best options are to bet or fold, not just call. Calling is weak. You're just reacting to someone else, so the only way you win is if you have the better hand. If someone's betting into you, that is no sure thing. This is one reason pros get so upset if they've lost a lot of money—or a tournament—"calling off my chips." It's a weak play.

Amateurs believe calling is an option between betting and folding on the value scale. Actually, calling is worse than folding because folding saves you money, while calling has shown weakness, which will make you a target and cost you money.

If you bet or raise, you give yourself an extra way to win. You know you can win with the best hand, but your aggression also allows you to win by making your foe fold a better hand or potential winner, either right now or on a later street. Pros seek this edge on every hand. That's why they'd rather fold than just call someone who will have control of the hand on the next round.

If you are going to call anyway, and you're not facing a raising hand, it's better to just bet rather than check and call

Besides having a monster, there are a few other times when you wouldn't bet a decent hand:

- You have a drawing hand and are trying to see cards cheaply, and betting will not enable you to bluff successfully if you miss.
- You have the lead, but there is a huge field against you that will likely overtake you, and betting will not get them to fold.
- You plan to check-raise or are trying to trap an aggressive player you know will bet into you.

As you can see, there are very few situations when you should not push the top hand. You should bet when you feel you are favored to win to make the pot larger. You must maximize profit from your winning hands (bet), and minimize losses from your losing ones (don't bet).

someone else's wager. But don't call just because you have put some chips in the pot. That money belongs to the pot now. And if you've made some mistakes in the hand, don't make it worse. Don't use a past bet to justify a future call.

Keep Them Guessing

You put your opponent to a decision by betting. Your bet must threaten him with the loss of something dear to him—his money—and he must know that future threats will be coming. He must know you as someone who isn't going to just fire one bullet—there's going to be a barrage. Now he's in the hot seat, not you.

POKER POINTER

If you consider not calling a bet because you are dwelling on what the money you are risking will buy, you are playing too high. If you risk any money not earmarked for "recreation," you are making a big mistake. Using that money will hurt your game and your life.

Good things happen when you bet. You establish a strong image, make opponents react to you, and take control. You give yourself multiple ways to win, and you get an idea of the strength of other hands. You force others to act. In return, you obtain information.

What's the worst that can happen? Someone has a hand? Then you fold. There's no shame in that—that's just being smart. But more often than not, he *won't* have a hand, but he will think *you* have one because you're putting your money where your mouth is and doing it strongly and fearlessly. However, a host of bad things occur if you just call or limp in:

- You lose control of the hand.
- You create a weak image.
- You don't drive others out of the pot.
- You invite bets and bluffs.
- You become a target on future streets.
- You allow drawing hands to beat you.

By just calling, you send a message that your hand is not to be feared. Unless you get real lucky, you're just throwing money away.

Hammer Your Foes with Raises

You can send a message with a bet, but a raise is a special delivery. If they still don't get it, a reraise or check-raise will hammer your point home like a telegram delivered by Sammy the Bull. There are tight games where raising is rare and reraising nonexistent, where players won't bet with A-K. You'll find aggressive games where folks not only raise with A-K, they will reraise with it or even cap the pot. It's all relative to the style of game and the hands your opponents are playing.

But one thing remains the same. A raise is a club you use to bludgeon your opponents who have popped their heads up into your line of fire by daring to bet. You slap them down with a raise. A raise can be so unexpected that the momentary unguarded look on your opponent's grill will tell you everything you need to know about his hand.

All that goes double for a reraise. A reraise (raising someone who's already raised) not only slaps him down, it stomps him into the dirt. Be careful with a reraise, though, if the person who raised you is the type to never bump it up without a huge hand.

ASK JOHNNY QUADS

What is the "nuts"?

The "nuts" is the best possible hand based on your cards and the cards of all the other players still in the hand. For example, if the board in Hold'em is 2-2-J-9-6, the best possible hand is four deuces—two deuces on the board and two deuces for someone's hole cards. If there are three spades on board and no pair, the nuts is an ace-high flush. Anyone with two spades in the hole, one of which is the ace, has the nuts.

Check-Raising

When you check and then raise when someone bets into you, that is a check-raise, and it can be the most devastating bet of all. A check-raise flat out tells the whole table that you have such a monster that you could afford to sit and wait for someone else to bet with the sole purpose of sucking more chips out of him. Its power is demoralizing and its element of surprise is devastating. This is so true that in tighter games, it can even be used as a bluff if you are against thinking players, as the check-raise is stating unequivocally that you have the nuts. The check-raise always gives away your hand, so decide first if it is the best way to maximize your profit or if you should be more straightforward.

The same can be said of the re-reraise. In most games, this would cap the pot, and in many games you won't get a cap without someone having pocket aces or sometimes kings preflop. A re-reraise is like a check-raise in that the re-reraiser is saying he has the nuts, and you should probably believe him. If you're in a position to cap it, think first. If it's not the river, sometimes it's best to hold back that last bet to disguise your hand and make more money on later streets, as long as your hand is not in danger.

It is important to make your opponents aware that you will check-raise and slow-play a big hand. If they don't believe you'll ever use these moves, then whenever you check, you invite an automatic bet from someone behind you.

POKER POINTER

"Tells" are cues shown by a player that either give away his hand (a big smile when he hits), some trickery (playing a hand differently than expected), a bluff (always tugging on an ear when he's lying), or his personality (counting his chips after every hand).

Send Out a Probe

Early in a hand, when the limits are lower, sending out a feeler bet will help you get a line on your opponent in a hurry. For example, say you have pocket kings in Hold'em. You've bet them preflop, have two callers, and then a dreaded ace flops with a six and a four. If you're first, you must bet. If you are raised, you have your answer—someone has aces. So you fold. If someone else bets first, and that isn't enough of a sign he has aces, then raise. If you are raised back, you know.

If someone tries to counter your probe by slow-playing, that's okay with you—you'll take a cheap card.

Bet On It!

All bets can bring you information, whether feelers, bluffs, or straight bets. Who's weak or strong in a specific hand is what you most want to know, but you also can get a line on who's weak or strong in general. Your bets are a less effective tool on those who won't be pushed around or intimidated. A good way to get an aggressive player off your back is just to push back, preferably with a hand, but if not, just betting back at him will put him on notice that you won't be run over.

You have to make a stand and show people you're willing to protect your turf. When you stand up, it is hoped you won't do it the one time the bully actually has a hand, so use your skills to pick a good spot—just don't wait too long to do it. And if you're in the lead, you must protect your hand. If you've bet preflop in Hold'em, you must in most cases bet after the flop. If you have the only pair on board in Stud, you have to bet it like you have two pair or trips—even if you have total hooey. If you don't, you should fold, because you've just told the table your hand sucks, and you will be run over.

If you detect weakness during a hand, you bet—no matter what you hold. If you detect weakness on the river, you bet to pick up the pot. Good players pound on weakness. It's like that in every sport. You must be the strong one, and in poker, betting is your weapon of strength. You use bets to manipulate how your hand is perceived, and it is the perception that counts. Other players will act according to their perception of your hand.

CHAPTER 7

POSITION AND ISOLATION

Position play and isolation are a poker player's mightiest tools. Position at the table is such a powerful advantage that a decent player with position on every hand would be virtually unbeatable, and a mediocre player with position would beat some pretty good pros. Mastering position play can help give you an edge on every hand.

What Is Position?

Your "position" is the point in the betting round when you must act relative to the other players. If there's a full table and you're one of the first to act, you're said to be in early position; if you're in the middle bunch, that's middle position; if you're in the final few, that's late position. Those who have acted before you are said to be in front of you, while those acting after you are behind you.

In some types of poker, your position will be fluid. With Stud, since the high card on the board bets first, you might be

89

in early position on one round, but if the player to your left suddenly gets high hand on board, you will be last to act. Position can be unpredictable as long as board cards are coming.

<u>**POKER POINTER**</u>

Since every bet, check, or raise sends out information, if you're last to act, you have it all spread out before you. Your opponents must cast their lot not knowing what you will do. By the time it's your turn, you will have analyzed their actions. The more players you have acting before you, and the fewer acting after, the more positional advantage you get.

But position play is most critical in community-card games. In Hold'em and Omaha, your position remains constant, which makes this another factor you have under control. If you start out in fourth position, you will stay in fourth position—until someone folds, of course. If you're on the button (the dealer), you're in last position, and everyone acts before you. And they will continue to act before you all hand long. If you're one of the blinds, you're in the earliest position, but in the first round, since you've already put money in, the third-position player is first. In later rounds, the blinds act first. Before the flop, the two players to the left of the blinds are considered in early position, the next three are in middle position, and the final three are late.

Late Position: A Good Place to Be

You're in the driver's seat in late position, especially if you're dead last. If you have a strong hand, someone may bet into you, so you hammer him with a raise, increasing your profit. Or someone may try to bluff, not having a clue that the last card made you strong. You make him pay. If those in front of you show weakness, then you try to buy the pot.

ASK JOHNNY QUADS

What is "sandbagging"?

Sandbagging is a slow-play strategy of "lying in the weeds," where a player doesn't bet a sure winning hand. Instead, he hopes another player will bet into him. Then he check-raises, and doubles his profit.

On the river, if your hand is borderline, you may be able to call without fearing a raise, and this could be the difference between winning and losing. If you are in middle position and call a bet, you risk a raise after you. You know that if someone raises, your hand is not a winner, so you've just thrown money away. If you're in late position, the borderline hands fear *you*. Strong late position hands get paid off more. In early position, if you bet your big hand, everyone may fold. In late position, someone may bet into you, or if it's checked to you and you bet, they may think you're just trying to buy the pot.

With starting hands, you're in the catbird seat. You can limp in with marginal hands on the end because you won't be raised, and during the hand you can get free cards when others fear a raise, or fold cheaply. In last position, you can check with less fear of others taking advantage of your weakness. As the hand progresses, you can give yourself free cards or call a bet without fear of a raise.

Are there any disadvantages to late position? Only the rare check-raise.

Early Position: All Eyes On You

While you're calm, cool, and collected in late position, early position is the opposite—a total nightmare. Take the best-case scenario: You have the nuts. Unfortunately, you're first to act. What do you do? If you bet, the others, thinking you must be super-strong to bet in early position, probably fold. Unlike late position, you have little chance of anyone betting into your monster. If you play it coy and sandbag it, the rest of the table might just check right along with you. Then you suffer the embarrassment of missing bets or, on the river, turning over the nuts without having made a bet.

At the other end of the spectrum, if you have a horrible hand, you won't have the option of bluffing on the river if everyone checks, as you would in late position. Where you travel the roughest road is with the borderline hands, those "possible" winners. Having little information, you will usually be stuck with a weak check, thus ensuring a bet from someone else. Then you're stuck again.

With borderline hands, not knowing others' strength makes you weak. You check much more than you should early in the hand, thus inviting people to run over you. You often violate the edict "Bet or fold, but don't just call," because you can't always risk a bet on just a "possible" winner with so many players still to act.

You can't play as many hands from early position, either. Starting hands that aren't worth a raise have to be thrown away, or you might find yourself in the untenable position of either putting in a bet and then having to fold, or wasting two or even three bets on a hand barely worth one, such as low pairs and low-suited connectors in Hold'em. Not knowing the number of opponents you'll be facing makes starting-hand decisions an expensive headache.

POKER POINTER

Whether to enter a hand in the first place is one of the most critical decisions in poker, and as much as any other factor—including the cards themselves—position determines which starting hands you should play.

There are many hands that might be worth calling a single bet with, but not two (such as 10-9 offsuit); and others that are worth a preflop call against a large field, but worthless against just a few opponents (3-3; 7-6 suited). In early position, you don't know the field size or if you will be raised, so you must dump many more hands.

Stealing Blinds, Stealing Pots

When it comes to taking control and reaping the financial rewards of that power, position is king. One of your key moves is stealing the blinds in late position, either on the button or one off. Raising to get the blinds to fold is essential if you have a good hand late, and just as essential if you have nothing and there is only one caller (or none) to you.

If you have a good hand late, you want the blinds out so they won't suddenly beat your A-Q by limping in with a trash hand and getting a low flop, like 8-6-3. Your A-Q doesn't look so good now, does it, if you let the blinds in free with their 7-5 or 8-2 or 6-5? If you bet again with that flop, a good player probably will call you down. You're going to need to pair up, and your chance of that is only 25 percent on the turn, 13 percent on the river.

Raising in Late Position

Get the blinds out at all costs. You know that if anyone called in front of you, they have some kind of hand, but you want the wild cards out—the blinds. If you allow them to limp in, they literally could have anything, which makes your post-flop decision a nightmare. If a blind bets right out after the flop, how can you call unless you hit a hand, which in most cases you will not? By being timid here, you've gone from favorite to underdog.

POKER POINTER

"Buying the button" is a sophisticated move that can get you position. If you are one or two to the right of the button, putting in a strong raise will often force the players after you to fold, giving you position on the rest of the field.

Raise at least three out of four times in late position unless there are many callers, and always if you have a hand and believe a raise will fold the blinds. The ideal scenario, though, is when there are few or no callers to you. Then you raise and steal the blinds. If they call, it's all right, because they will now understand that you will make this bet whether you have a top hand or not. This gets your better hands paid off. If you get called, so what? You have position on the next round, when you *should* bet again, unless you feel it in your bones that you're facing a hand. In that case, maybe you'll get a free card. If someone bets into you, you can easily fold. No harm done.

Stealing the blinds is your gateway to stealing pots. You've built an image as being a little reckless by always betting in the last two positions, when in fact it's a calculated move and you are anything but loose. Advertising this play can only help get your big hands called. Not making this move could have the opposite effect: You will be perceived as weak.

Do Your Opponents Know Position?

The value of position grows with the stakes. When big money is at risk, every edge is magnified. At higher limits, many players are rock solid as far as position, particularly when it comes to starting hands. Fortunately, this makes them somewhat predictable. It is easier to put them on hands. You know there are hands they simply will not play in certain positions. That's the good news. The bad news is the hands you put them on are usually quite formidable.

POKER POINTER

There is a time-tested truism in poker that you should "sit behind the money." In other words, have the players with the most chips on your right. This is because during a game, money flows in a clockwise direction, and those with the most power will act before you.

At lower stakes, many players won't understand position, and they'll play the same hands from anywhere. It is up to you to spot these players and adjust. As a fringe benefit, you'll have them betting right into the teeth of your big hands.

Even in a wild game, position will help you. You won't be able to steal pots, but with good position you can observe all the craziness and then simply fold. When you have a great hand, you can hammer those who made the loose bets earlier. In a tight game, you can kill people with position bets. If the world's biggest rock finally bets, you can quietly fold from late position without giving him or her a cent.

Curiously, in early position, the strategy is similar in both loose and tight games: check and fold a lot of hands.

The Concept of Isolation

The more you play, the more you will realize that your lead in a hand is hanging by a slender thread, and even the best starting hands are vulnerable. This is the case in Stud, where you receive 43 percent of your total cards before you must act (three of seven), but it's especially true in Hold'em, where you start with only two (28 percent). This makes the game highly unpredictable. Even with great pocket cards, a lot of water has to go under the bridge before you bring that pot home.

With the exception of small pairs and straight and flush draws (where you often wish to chase a longshot payoff against a large field), starting hands in Hold'em demand isolation. You must thin the field. Sure, if you have a high rolled-up set in Stud or aces in Hold'em against rocks, you may want to be coy, but even aces will only win 34 percent of the time against nine random hands, and 44 percent of the time against six. The second-best hand, pocket kings, is also vulnerable. If you don't believe that, let people in cheaply sometime and see how you feel when an ace flops. You now have just two outs and an 8-percent chance of winning, all because you got greedy and let someone in cheap with A-4, instead of forcing a fold.

Multiple Opponents Are Powerful

The more overcards there are to your hand, the more tenuous your lead. If you have A♠-10♠ and the flop is 10♥-9♥-3♣, you have to bet like crazy. If you have the chance to make it two bets to go, do so. There are three overcards to your ten that will kill you, and the larger the field against you, the greater the chance that someone will hit. For example, if the players against you combined have a jack, queen, and king, all of which beat you if paired, they have nine outs and a 35-percent chance of hitting by the river. If someone has Q-J or J-8 for a straight draw, you can add four more outs, making thirteen. Now your chance of winning is down to 52 percent. If someone's paired the board (J-9), that's trouble, as there's now a two-pair draw, and if there's a flush draw as well (e.g., K♥-Q♥), you are now at least a 2-to-1 *underdog* to win. You could have this whole arsenal against you in the hands of only three foes!

POKER POINTER

To "straddle," the player to the left of the big blind puts up double the big blind's "bet"; in other words, he "raises" the big blind before he's been dealt a hand. The player to the straddle's left is now first to act, and the "straddler" may raise his own bet when the action comes around to him.

When you are in the lead, you must look at the field cumulatively. You don't treat adversaries as separate entities and say, "I have the best hand." You might very well have the best hand, and the best chance of winning against any *one* of them, but against the *field* you will lose more often than not. Still, you absolutely must bet strongly and make them pay for the privilege of trying to beat you. That is one of the principles of good poker.

Isolate Early and Often

Isolation begins with your starting hand. You must get the field down to a manageable number so that when you have top pair on the flop (the most likely way you'll be in the lead), you can drive it home. Betting before the flop sets up plays *on* the flop. That's why if you bet preflop, you should almost always bet post-flop. Get others in the habit of seeing you do this. This is an expected play. It makes sense: If you are strong before the flop, you want them to think you are strong after as well. If you show weakness here, you invite rout, and having a small field is advantageous on every street. Naturally, you must examine your options if you meet resistance, but if you have top pair on the flop—either with tens, as in the previous example, or with an overpair like pocket jacks to the 10-9-3 flop—you must make it as expensive as possible for those draws to chase.

It is an overlooked concept that the more players there are in a hand, the better hand you will need to win. This begins with the starting hands and is true all the way to the river. In a heads-up game, you don't need much. But in an eight- or ten-player game, you need a *very* good hand. The chance of someone getting pocket aces in a ten-player game is 22-1 against; in heads-up, it's 110-1. It's 8-1 against any one of the ten players being dealt A-K, but it's a 41-1 shot heads-up. (In Seven-Stud, odds are 5-1 against being dealt a pair in the opening three cards. In an eight-person game, you can be sure someone will have one, but in heads-up, the odds say neither will have a pair.)

The more players at the table, the better the chance *someone* has a top starting hand. The more players, the more hands seeing the flop, and the better those hands are. And with more seeing the flop (or fourth street in Stud), there are many more combinations to fear.

Who to Target for Isolation

Some players are just asking for you to get them alone. The following player types are the most vulnerable, if you have any kind of early hand at all:

- **Wild players.** You build on their raises by reraising, making it too expensive for others to stay. You know they have nothing, so your raise not only isolates them, it allows you to bet them out of the pot if they don't get lucky on the flop or turn.
- **Loose players.** Since you know they stay with many mediocre hands in all positions, if you can isolate them, your higher card—any ace, king, or even queen—should make you the favorite over their 10-8, J-9, 9-8, and all the small suited hands they love to play.
- **Poor players.** Any time you can get it heads-up against an inferior or inexperienced player, you're the favorite.

They play poorer quality hands, don't understand isolation, and have trouble discerning your hand. Your raise puts them on the defensive, and they will often fold if they don't hit top pair.

- **Straddlers.** Raising without seeing their cards—what are these players thinking? You know full well the odds are against them being dealt a hand, so you bet it up with anything to isolate them preflop. Then just drive their trash out.

The best way to isolate someone is if you can raise or—even better—reraise her. If you can make it two or three bets to go to the rest of the field, you'll get it heads-up most of the time.

Isolation in Action

Here's a typical example of why you must isolate with most top hands. You have A-Q preflop. You believe it's the best hand. Heads-up you're in good shape, but against three players you win just 39 percent of the time, and 25 percent against six. The problem is the flop—your chance of pairing is just 3 in 10. This is okay against one player—you can still bet whether you hit or not because you can assume he hasn't improved either. But facing three or more, you know someone's paired and has you beat. Your chance of pairing on the turn or river is only 24 percent, so unless he's a weak player, you must check and fold.

The second example is going all-in with a big bet in no-limit or pot-limit—the quintessential isolation play. If you have lowly pocket deuces and can get it heads-up, you're actually a slight favorite against all other hands except higher pairs—even A-K! If you had to play limit through four betting rounds, however, the A-K would kill the deuces, because all the overcards would either get them beat outright or prevent them calling all the way.

Take the third example. You have pocket nines. Unless you want to just limp in and hope for trips against a large field, you know your only chance is to get it heads-up, so you bet it up preflop. Of course, a favorable flop, like 8-6-2, would give you an overpair. But heads-up, unless the flop is scary (like A-K-J, and so on), you can count on your opponent missing the flop. Then you bet him out. But since at least one overcard will flop 69 percent of the time (when you don't flop a set), with *multiple* opponents, someone's going to pair up and beat you.

Setting a Trap

In no-limit poker, trapping is king. It's all about waiting for someone to go all-in against your hidden monster hand, playing some cards others might not expect, and buying pots with big bets while praying that this time, you aren't betting into the nuts.

Slow-Playing: Risks and Reward

In limit poker, your traps aren't as deadly, but they are no less essential because your opponents must know you are capable of setting them. Trapping, more often called "slow-playing" in limit, brings an element of unpredictability to your game that keeps foes guessing. When a player bets little or nothing on his strong hand to disguise its strength, hoping to make other players overvalue their hands and pay him off handsomely, he is slow-playing. When you check your big hand, you're just begging someone to try to buy the pot. Then it's check-raise time!

Slow-Playing the Big Pairs

Getting a wired pair (pocket pair) of either aces or kings is a 110-to-1 shot, so you want to make sure you make hay when you get 'em. This means that *sometimes* you will slow-play early. You don't want *everyone* to fold if you bet preflop. You'd like to thin the field to two or three foes. With more than three, there is too much risk of someone hitting a crazy flop. One opponent might just fold if he misses the flop, but with two or three, someone could catch a pair or a draw and he'll pay you off.

POKER POINTER

A "big pair" means aces or kings here, not queens or below. With queens, there is a 31-percent chance of an overcard hitting the flop (when you don't flop a set), and that spells trouble if you slow-played. With kings, a dreaded ace will flop only 12 percent of the time (with no set). If that's still too scary, then only slow-play aces, and bet strong on the rest.

Here's a big note of caution. Limit poker is still about thinning the field and betting your leading hands. Resist the home-game "strategy" of always going for the big score, unless you're a mortal lock. With trapping, you always are weighing the payoff versus the risk of letting others stay in the hand.

CHAPTER 8

WHEN, HOW, AND WHO TO BLUFF

When you use aggressive betting with the best hand to isolate opponents, you are in poker paradise because you are being honest. But poker becomes difficult when you do not want foes to know your cards. Knowing what you're holding allows them to make correct decisions when you want them to make mistakes. So you use misdirection and deception to keep your cards secret. The ultimate deceptive play is the bluff: a gutsy move where you bet a whole bunch of chips—on nothing!

The Art of Misdirection

Bluffing is a move that resonates throughout the game, and sometimes games to come, but it is no easy trick. In fact, many players just can't bring themselves to try it, and those are the players doomed forever to mediocrity. You bluff by risking money, sometimes lots of it. There's no way around that. But it is a move that every poker player must make, whether it is successful or not. Bluffing can be profitable even when it fails, because it sticks in the minds of your opponents like glue.

ASK JOHNNY QUADS

What is a poker face?

A poker face is the countenance every player "puts on" to conceal his emotions, his thoughts, and his cards during a poker hand, but it is not a robotic mask. A good poker face is natural, relaxed, and reveals nothing, even if the player makes a royal flush—or misses one.

Poker is the only game where the best hand doesn't always win—that is why it is called a "psychological" game, and why "people" players usually beat "mathematical" players. Your hand is as good as your determination to back it up. If you know what makes your opponents tick, you can figure what they're holding and use their actions to read their thoughts and predict their responses. Then you can choose the optimal time to bluff. If the bluff is successful, your opponents will drop their cards like hot potatoes, and you will take the pot with a worse hand. If the bluff is unsuccessful, your foes are on notice that you will try anything—and could do it again.

The Benefits of the Bluff

Bluffing is the essence of poker. Without the twin threats of bluffing and monetary loss, the game is incredibly boring. It is so important that even in games where it is very difficult to bluff successfully, bluffing remains one of the most profitable moves in poker. Why? Because without bluffing, you are an open book.

Unpredictability

Bluffing makes you unpredictable and disguises your future hands. If others know you bluff and will risk money on less than the best hand, they will pay you off when you get those nut hands. You know how frustrating it is to get that monster and win nothing. If that happens frequently, you're just not bluffing enough, so *advertise* that you bluff. When you get caught, announce that you have nothing. Show your hand. The money you paid for this "ad campaign" will return big dividends, because it will help "sell" your big hands later.

Bluffing gives you that elusive "second way" to win a hand. You don't have to hold the best cards to grab the pot. But unless you're against the world's weakest players, you aren't going to bluff all the time. You bluff until you are caught, then pick your spots. You know they will start calling you more once they know you try to buy pots. When they get in the calling mode, shift gears and start playing top hands. After beating their brains out with top hands, they'll start folding again. At that point, you can start bluffing again. Pretty soon they won't know if they're coming or going—they will be guessing, and usually guessing wrong.

The Worst Case

Compare the bluffing scenario to what happens if you do *not* bluff. First, since opponents know you will never bet on a hand you do not believe in, they soon will cop to what hands you like. If you play some questionable cards, they will take advantage of that. If you only play top hands, they will quickly fold when you bet—except when someone else has a monster hand, in which case he will beat your brains in. To say you are predictable would be an understatement. Since you never bluff, you won't get called on the river unless someone has you beat. You can't figure out why you never win the big pots.

It all boils down to this: Opponents must believe that your bets do not always mean what they say. That is how you get action on your good hands. But it is a fine line you must walk. You know you must be able to drive people out and thin the field on some hands. Remember, your bets must be respected, so you can use them like a hammer when you need to bet drawing hands out of the pot, isolate, or get it heads-up (and yes, bluff successfully). Think "shock and awe" here. Therefore, you can't be constantly bluffing or playing foolishly. Foes should just have a subtle awareness that "this person will bluff" somewhere in the backs of their minds.

Aggressive Play

Since you will bluff until you are caught, you will be caught. Once discovered with your hand in the cookie jar, your opponents will call you more often. But how do you reconcile bluffing, which encourages future calls, with your desire to have your bets respected, so you can protect your tenuous leads and force people to fold when you don't have a lock?

The answer is to be aggressive from the start in the hands you have carefully chosen to play—bluffing or not. Plain and simple, your opponents must know that it will cost them dearly to call you. If you are in a hand, you will be betting. Sometimes you may not have it, but sometimes you will. Either way, they are going to have to invest some serious money to find out.

What if you are played back at, and someone has put *you* to the test? Here is where knowing your players will save you. What hand is he representing? Does he have it? Does the way he has played the hand support it? Has he caught on to your aggressive style and is now trying to take the play away from you with trash, or is he a rock who finally has a hand? Your people skills will tell you whether to raise back or to back off. Remember, there's no shame in folding. Losing a little skirmish is okay, as long as you win the big battles.

Control, Intimidation, and Confusion

If you are aggressive *and* winning, others will back off. You're in control. Someone might even whisper in your ear, "They're afraid of you." You're intimidating. The bad players will just be confused, the better ones will go into a shell until they figure you out, and the rocks will get "rockier"—just waiting for those monster hands that never come.

ASK JOHNNY QUADS

What is a "maniac"?

In poker, a maniac is a loose, aggressive player who wreaks havoc in a game by making a lot of bets with questionable cards. Because his aggressiveness is not selective and he doesn't know when to back off, he loses a lot of chips to rocks who trap him with strong hands.

Now you have two decisions. First is finding the proper moment to shift gears into a more conservative style, and second is determining whether they think you are aggressive in a calculated, intelligent way, or just a maniac. If it's the former, they will sit and wait for good cards. Someone may make a run at you to test you, but you'll be ready for that. If they think you're a maniac making a lot of loose bets on average hands, the better players may challenge you and try to isolate you.

An Aggressive Move

Being aggressive is more than just making a bunch of bets. Others must view the bets as powerful. If you're facing someone who's challenging you, bet him back down. Raising the raiser will quickly tell you what you're facing, and isolate. And check-raising, of course, is saying in no uncertain terms, "I have a monster hand."

Many new players will make the following play. They flop a top hand, like a set, and then check to the preflop bettor. They plan to check-raise when he bets. This often works, but you've told the bettor you have a monster. He'll now fold, or see the turn and fold. But if you *bet into the bettor*—bet first— he now very well might raise you (as long as you haven't given away that you're unbeatable). Then you can either raise back, or just call him and suck more money out of him on the turn. If it's more action you're seeking, betting into the bettor is usually the more professional play.

When to Bluff

When bluffing, timing is everything. Mathematical players might tell you a bluff is recommended when pot odds warrant it. If your odds are 1 in 4 of being successful with your $20 bluff, but there is a $100 pot, you're getting 5-1 on your money. That's 5-1 on a 3-1 shot! It's a profitable play, if your assessment is correct. That, of course, is the tough part: predicting if those with better hands will call. Here are a few factors to consider when deciding when to bluff:

- **The size of the pot.** After the pot grows past a certain point, the pot odds are so great for a caller that he's not going to just let you walk off with it.
- **The number of players in the hand.** The more players, the greater the chance that someone is going to have a hand good enough to call, or even call just for the heck of it.
- **The personality of the players against you.** There are some who just will not let someone take a pot uncontested and would rather waste chips than risk being bluffed out.
- **Did everyone show weakness?** If the whole table has checked, you almost are forced to bluff, if only to protect your future winning hands, especially on the river.
- **What hands have you put people on?** During the hand, you figured players for certain cards. Did they hit? How many have you beat? Are their hands good enough to call?
- **Is one of your opponents loose or on tilt?** If so, what was his past performance on the river? Does he check-raise? Does he call on the river "just in case"?
- **Has a scare card just hit the board?** Has a card just shown up that you know will scare your foes, like

pairing your door card in Stud, or an ace or third flush card in Hold'em?

- **What is your history in the hand?** Have you shown any strength? Have you just checked along, or acted like it was your pot? Do they fear you now, or will your bluff be "out of the blue?"
- **What are the sizes of the stacks against you?** Those with huge stacks (big winners) and those down to almost nothing (big losers) are often more inclined to call than others.
- **Have your bets been getting called lately, especially on the river?** If everyone has been folding, you have not been bluffing enough. This is the ideal time to start doing it.
- **Are you known as a maniac, bluffer, or loose player?** If so, you will be called for sure.

Unless you have a line on your opponents' holdings, it's difficult to calculate if your bluff has a chance. Of course, if anyone has a line on your style, or if you cannot bet your bluff in exactly the same manner as you would a genuine hand, then your bluff will fail. In general, the larger the pot, the harder it is to bluff successfully. The lower the stakes, the harder it is to pull it off. And, believe it or not, the *less* savvy your opponents, the harder it is to bluff them out.

Try the "Semi-Bluff"

A semi-bluff is betting when you are behind in the hand, but you have outs. You can win if you hit your hand, but you can also win because your opponents may put you on a made hand, and they may fold to your river bet even if you don't hit. Here are some examples.

You have raised the blinds preflop with A-Q and have three callers. The flop comes 10-8-5. You bet it, and two people call. You don't believe they paired up, but if they did, you still have two overcards. You're going to figure them for a straight draw or overcards not as high as yours. Although you have only a 24-percent chance to make a pair, you have control of the hand. Unless the turn is a king or a jack (and sometimes even then), you will bet the turn and drive them out. If someone is still around, you'll fire another bullet on the river.

In the above example, if your ace and queen were both spades, and the ten and the eight were both spades, you now have fifteen outs, or a 54-percent chance of hitting by the river. Just bet like you have something, all the way. If you don't make it, you might win with a final bet on the river. Betting with an overcard (or underpair) along with a straight or flush draw is a very sound semi-bluff.

POKER POINTER

In addition to its other benefits, a semi-bluff can be odds correct. If you have more callers (say, five) than your odds of hitting a nut draw (such as 4-1), your bet is a long-term moneymaker.

Another Semi-Bluff

You call a preflop raise in late position with 10-9 suited. The flop is J-8-5 rainbow. There are two checks and a bet to you. You raise it. The two checks fold, and the raiser calls.

He has at most jacks, maybe eights, but more likely just an ace and decent kicker. If he has A-J, you figure, he would've reraised. With eight outs to the nut straight, the odds are more than 2-to-1 against you, but by taking control, you might win anyway. If he just has overcards, he has to hit one of his six outs or fold to your aggression. You'll bet it right out if he checks the turn, and the large turn bet might get him to fold right there. If he bets, you'll definitely call because you have the odds to chase your draw. If you think he's just feeling you out, this is an advanced play. Is he that good? You could reraise him to find out, but if he calls, you can be sure he'll call the river as well, so you're cooked if you don't hit. If he reraises, you're cooked unless you hit your draw. If he only calls your turn bet, you'll fire another shot at the river, whether you hit the straight or not.

The beauty is you have outs—it's not just a bluff and a prayer. Do you see how you'd be in even better position psychologically if you had raised preflop? That's why they say, "If you're going in, go in raising!" With semi-bluffs, think in your mind that you've already made a hand, and bet accordingly, with confidence and power.

What Hand Does He Think You Have?

Always keep in mind how you are perceived and what hand your opponent is putting *you* on. In the last example, what hand could you have that could scare him out? You want him to think A-J or a set, which would beat his K-J, Q-J, J-10, or A-8. Bluffing is rarely effective if you can't *represent* something. Ideally, you want to represent a specific card. Opponents need something tangible to fear. The bet has to make sense and be logical and plausible. It's hard to fear a flop like 8-7-3. What could you have? But if the flop is Q-Q-8, they will fear a queen. If you bet right out, they might believe you, depending on how you would play if you actually had it. Do you see how playing "made" hands coyly can backfire? If you always bet your hands, then when you bluff here, they will think you could have trips. But if you would always check the queens to trap (check-raise) someone, then you can't bluff, because your normal play would be a "check" here! And if you check and someone else bets, you must fold.

POKER POINTER

There's a saying in Hold'em about when a scary high pair flops, as with J-J-9: "It isn't the person who bets who has trips, it's the person who calls." Beware of the quiet ones in this situation. This is a rare time when a check-raise bluff might work—just be careful if you're called. You might be facing a real hand!

For a bluff to work, what you represent has to conform to the betting pattern during the hand—therefore, you rarely just suddenly decide to throw in a bluff bet on the river. You must be thinking ahead, setting it up. If the bet pattern doesn't compute, someone's going to smell a rat and call.

"Betting like you have it" is an aggressive way of playing drawing hands. The other way of playing draws is to get in as cheaply as humanly possible, since most times you won't make it. Semi-bluffing gives you another way to win for all those times, and it takes care of the problem of "setting up" your bluff during the hand because you'll bet all the way. Vary your play from one strategy to the other.

Who to Bluff

In many respects the perfect opponent is one who has no clue what is going on. But this isn't the case when it comes to bluffing. Why? You can't bluff a monkey! You cannot represent a hand to someone who doesn't think about your hand, only his own. With someone who just puts in chips because he feels like it, you're just going to have to beat him with good hands, which he will pay off handsomely.

POKER POINTER

Bluffing may sound risky, but put yourself in your opponent's shoes. When you bet early and strongly, he figures he's going to have to call all the way to the river to find out if you're bluffing. But you're in a much better spot: You can call it off at any time. Since you can fold after firing just one shot, you have much less at risk than he does.

Now, good players—they can be bluffed. Sounds strange, but it's true. They can also catch on when you are bluffing if you're not careful. Unlike bad players, who don't fold enough, good players can even fold winning hands. It happens, and that's okay. No one can call all the time. That's weak. Sometimes, in tennis, a shot will be just "too good." There's no defense for it. No need to chase the shot. Some bets in poker are like that, too—just "too good." It's the perfect bet in the perfect spot, and it can't be called. If someone has bluffed, good for him. Only a fool is a calling station who pays off hand after hand just to keep from being bluffed once in a while.

You calculate how your foe will analyze the hand, and if your betting matches the hand he puts you on, and that hand is probable and would beat him, he's going to fold. But you must be facing someone who can think intelligently about a hand, and *you* must have a reputation as a solid player—not too loose, and not a flake. So ask yourself, "Who's paying attention?"

Let's Talk Risk

It's a general rule of poker not to risk a lot to win a little. For example, it's a foolish move in no-limit to put in a ton of chips just to win the blinds. Sooner or later, someone's going to have a hand and take you down. But it is perfectly correct to bluff at the blinds in both limit and no-limit poker. It's a high-percentage play that will win the pot immediately or after the flop if you bet then. And if someone wants to bluff at a tiny pot, and you're not sure whether to call, just give it to him.

Bluffing and Position

Running a bluff in late position after others have checked is expected, but doing it from early position can sometimes work because it's so gutsy. If everyone has checked (or at least not raised) on the turn and a weak card hits the river, try betting right out from early position. Good players know you're not going to bet early unless you really have something because there are so many to act after you, so they might overvalue your hand. You just might buy the pot. In a weak hand, the first person to bet often wins.

Should You Call a Possible Bluff?

The math players have a simple formula for calling. If the pot odds are greater than the chance he's bluffing, then call. For example, if the pot is $50 and the bet is $10, you're getting 5-to-1 on your money. But the player almost never bluffs. You figure it's 10-1 against him bluffing here. So you'll lose $100 and win $50 in eleven tries, for a net loss of $50. But if he's a known bluffer, you might figure he'll bluff once out of five times he's faced with this situation. In this case, you lose $40 but win $50 in five tries by calling, for a gain of $10. A good bet.

The courage to "bet on nothing" comes from understanding the game, while fear comes from the unknown. The more you play, the more comfortable you will become, and the confidence to run killer bluffs will follow.

CHAPTER 9

OTHER PLAYERS
TELL ALL

A tell is the unintentional giveaway of a player's personality, playing style, or hand. Tells can be facial expressions, revealing mannerisms, body language, gestures, movements, speech patterns, breaks in routine, conscious acts meant to mislead, or unconscious bodily responses to stress. You must observe and analyze. If you are superior to your adversaries at spotting tells (and hiding your own), you are on the path to victory.

Tells Reveal Deception

To discover tells, you must become a human lie detector. As with the machine, you must first establish what is normal behavior for your subject. Since poker is a game of deception, it will not be easy to find your foe in a natural, unguarded moment, but it can be done. Watch him when he's not in a hand. Engage him in conversation, and observe his demeanor. Watch how he acts during play when he is telling the truth: betting it up when he has a big hand, for example, or acting as if he missed a draw and following that with a "true" action—folding. Next, try to pick up when he is being deceptive. How does his demeanor change when he has a great hand, good hand, bad hand, or bluffing hand? To be successful, a player can't give away his cards or let someone know when he's got the nuts, so he often acts weak to get a bigger payoff. And he never wants his enemies to know when he's weak, or they will bet him out of a hand he so dearly wants to play, so he will act strong.

POKER POINTER

If you think you've discovered a tell, never let that player just muck his hand if he has called on the river and been beaten. Ask to see his hand, and remember how he played it, his mannerisms and how he looked during the hand. Without seeing the cards, you cannot be sure that you have found a genuine tell.

This deception, which at its core is "fibbing without words," creates tension that reaches its zenith during a big bluff on the river or an all-in bet in no-limit. But any deception, in a way, can be considered a bluff—a lie. The subterfuge creates changes that can be measured by the lie detector, or you. (The one exception to this would be a semi-bluff, where a player does not have the best hand but is comfortable with his play, because he still has outs and is getting sufficient odds from the pot.)

What good poker players realize is that the struggle to hide deception creates internal conflict that manifests itself in involuntary responses in the body, which are sometimes observable. Detecting them is part of your winning strategy. You also must discover deliberate attempts to mislead you. Tells are the keys that unlock these doors of deception.

Unconscious Tells

"Unconscious" or "reflex" tells are not deliberate. Like a dog wagging his tail when he's happy, your opponents may not be aware of them at all. And if they are, they may be powerless to stop those telltale responses and only mildly successful at hiding them. Some involuntary tells include the following:

- **Sweating.** Obviously a sign of nervousness.
- **Sudden leg shaking.** Another nervous signal.
- **Trembling hands.** Not always a nervous sign.
- **Sudden dilation of pupils.** She likes what she sees.
- **Sitting at attention.** Why is he doing this now?
- **Not breathing.** Why isn't she? She's not dead.
- **Croaky voice.** He can barely get a word out.
- **Suddenly quiet.** The table "talker" is abruptly silent.

When you see an opponent exhibit one of these tells, your work is just beginning. Since some of these are a sign of tension, not trickery, you have the same problem as the lie-detector operator. Is the "lying" response the result of nerves, or actual deception?

To answer this question, you must study your opponents—when you're in a hand *and* after you've folded. For example, with the sweating type, ask yourself if he always sweats or if it just happens at certain times. Then see if it's apparent when he's bluffing or on a draw, as opposed to when he's got the nuts. If it's one or the other, and it's repeated, you may have a usable tell.

Some players will be just as nervous when they have a monster hand and are praying someone will call as when they are on a stone bluff. This is why you verify tells before you spend money on them.

You can avoid nervousness after making a big bet by being "one" with your decision. The tough part is over—the time leading up to your action. Regardless of the outcome, have faith that you made the correct play. Be serene and don't look back.

Some Reliable Tells

When you notice a player suddenly sitting up straight, watch out. He usually has a hand. In general, watch for posture that says "I'm interested" right from the get-go. Good posture, leaning into the table, or a sudden posture shift are all indicators of strength. You'll have to pay attention to see this one, but how about the guy or gal who bets and doesn't take a breath? It's obvious something's going on here. Is she bluffing, or hoping for a call because she's a lock? This one is almost always a bluff, but again, study the players for verification. If you've put your opponent on a hand during earlier streets, your decision will be easier when that big river bet or raise punches you in the grill, because you can compare the river card to what you believe your opponent is holding.

Those on a total bluff have steeled themselves for the jitters and stare-downs, so they often appear calm—so calm they can hardly breathe, their bodies are rigid, and their faces are made of stone! It's unnatural—a probable bluff.

If you can engage players in conversation before you make a tough decision, you'll be surprised at how difficult it is for them to talk if they are stressed. Sometimes the words come out as a hoarse croak, as if they have stage fright or have been called to the principal's office. Generally, the throaty rasp of a dry mouth indicates a bluff more than a monster. Those who can talk naturally here are truly a step ahead.

ASK JOHNNY QUADS

What is the "rail"?

The "rail" is the velvet rope or railing that separates the people watching a game from those actually playing poker. The watchers are called *railbirds*, a pathetic lot reduced to plaintively asking for money to get back in action as players walk by to go to the bathroom.

Think about this if you're ever in a no-limit tournament and someone's just made an all-in bet that could bust you, and he is staring you down like a statue: If you can get the bettor to talk, who knows what information might come spilling out—not in the words, but in the way they are said. Logic says a person with a cinch hand will be more at ease. So if the serenity doesn't "ring true," it means a bluff.

Talking: A Dead Giveaway

Only the most experienced of players can babble away without giving something up, and then only if talking is their strategy. There are players who can talk others out of their game—get them so off-stride, distracted, and frustrated that they practically go on tilt. There are others who deliberately bait people, criticize someone's play, or even bring up religion or politics to annoy others to the point that they cannot concentrate.

POKER POINTER

The old expression "Loose lips sink ships" is certainly true in poker. You can give it all away to an astute listener through subtle, uncontrollable changes in tempo, tone, pitch, or even content. And since shutting up is the deadest giveaway of all, talkers need to keep talking. For "normal" players, the more you talk, the more you give away.

But those who can talk a good game without revealing something are few—so many words coming out, and each one a potential clue! Pay attention. It may seem like an endless stream of nonsense, but the blather is loaded with hidden meaning. It is difficult for a nonstop talker to look at his hand without giving something away in his inflection or with a hesitation. Betting is doubly hard. If he gets a hand, he'll momentarily be on overload as he decides what to do. Listen for the hesitation, even a momentary stutter.

A Bluffing-Tell Quandary

There is a tell that has become so well-known it has taken on a life of its own, and it illustrates the type of double- and triple-think that takes place among well-read players. The scenario revolves around the classic desire of players to appear strong when weak, and weak when strong, and it concerns those who are staring at you—hard—especially if they've put in a big bet and you're considering calling. The intense gaze was either supposed to make you wither and fold, or figure that the bettor could not make such lengthy eye contact if he was bluffing.

And there certainly is some truth to that. Many liars (bluffers) cannot look someone in the eye. It is often a legitimate tell (except among practiced poker players). Therefore, if the bettor was giving you the stare-down, it must follow that he had the good hand he was representing. So you fold. Right?

Not so fast. If he is aware of that thinking, then he will stare you down through an effort of will. He has nothing (weak), but is representing strength with intimidating eye contact, daring you to call. Here is where top player/author/lecturer Mike Caro comes in. His groundbreaking *Book of Tells*, published in 1984, is still the definitive work on the subject. In it, he states, "Players staring at you are usually less of a threat than players staring away."

POKER POINTER

In a pivotal hand of the 2003 World Series of Poker final table, eventual winner Chris Moneymaker bluffed out seasoned pro Sam Farha, who ignored two obvious tells: first, Chris stared him down after his all-in bet, and second, Chris put his hand over his mouth—a classic sign of deception.

Players staring away are nonconfrontational, passive—"not a problem." They are representing weakness, the thinking goes, and therefore they are strong, for rarely would someone deliberately represent weakness if he was in fact weak. Players staring at you want you to feel strength and back off. Someone with a very good hand wouldn't want you to back off, so he must be weak.

Now, two decades later, the "staring-at-you-means-weak" tell has been so publicized that many are back to staring at you with big hands again. They stare at you, you think they're weak, you call or raise, and—wham!—they put the nuts on you. Go figure!

Study Your Opponents

Experts have their bodies under control and are skilled at appearing natural. You won't find them sweating, shaking, or croaking. Sure, it's unnatural to be perfectly calm in a pressure situation, but top players can sublimate the tension, and they are used to the mental conflict of deception. The stress will manifest itself, but in ways too subtle for most to notice.

At the same time, the experts will be deliberately deceptive to steal a pot that is rightfully yours. But all is not lost. Their moves require action, and within every action hides a tell. Subtle, perhaps, but still there. You uncover the deceit by smoking out what he wants you to believe and what action he really wants you to perform, and then doing the opposite.

Make a List, Check It Twice

A major weapon is a mental rundown of who the deceptive players are at your table. Observe the game closely. Ask to see called hands. Some folks will never represent a hand they don't really have. It's just too much trouble. This might cost them some bets, but for them, to be free of mental conflict is worth it. Then there are those who are deceptive in certain situations. They'll run a play once or twice in position. And, of course, there are the dangerous players—those who are a threat to steal on every hand. If you give them an inch, they'll take the pot.

Hold'em Illustration

Say you have Q-J in Hold'em. You and three others see the flop without a raise, which is Q-10-7 rainbow. Two players check to you, you bet, and the player behind you raises. The two checkers fold. What do you do? Here's where your list is a lifesaver. If the raiser is a tight player, you know full well he has at least a queen, and he probably wouldn't play a queen with a lower kicker than yours. The fact that there was no preflop raise and he was on the button is your only hope. If there had been a preflop raise, you would be 100 percent certain the rock has a better hand than you. (See the value of raising preflop in late position?) You could reraise, and then if he raised you back (unlikely for a rock), you fold. But if he calls, then what do you do? You risk a check-raise on the turn or a sure bet if you check. Best option is to either fold right now, or check and call him all the way to the river to see if you are beaten. But wait! When he raised you, he did it with authority. You know from playing with him for five hours that he only does this when he has a real hand. Is this the one time all night he's crossing you up? Don't bet on it! Fold with confidence.

There's a big difference if the raiser is on your "loose" list or is habitually deceptive. A deceptive player expects others to chronically steal and bluff just like he does, so he won't give you credit for a hand. He might raise just to "bluff the bluffer." So you reraise him for sure. At best, he has a queen with a worse kicker than you, or a draw. He's a guy who would automatically raise preflop on the button into three limpers with almost anything. You figure him for an ace or second or third pair, perhaps J-10, K-7, or A-7.

ASK JOHNNY QUADS

What kind of expression should I have at the table?

The best poker face appears confident, natural, and doesn't give anything away when the cards hit. Show the countenance of a warrior: strong, smart, and ready, and ruled by neither anger nor passivity.

There's one caution, and here is where your tell-reading comes in. Did he slow-play a real hand (A-Q, K-Q, aces, kings, queens, tens) on the button? The only thing that will save you in this situation is if you know this player! The moral is this: The odds can give you the probability that you're beat, but with a tell, you can be certain.

Catch Them with Their Guard Down

Players give away their hands most often in the instant they see cards for the first time and when they must take some overt action, such as betting. Watch your opponents' eyes, faces, hands, and bodies at these crucial moments:

- The first time they look at their hole cards. Recall their reactions to different hands.

- When they look at their last hole card (Stud). Watch others, not your own hand.
- When the flop is turned over. Look at others, not the cards. You can peek later.
- When the turn is exposed, then the river—especially the critical final card.

Once you have noted players' responses to the cards, compare them to the final hands turned over on the river. Caution: Try to hide that you're watching! And as for yourself, train yourself not to react. Use the same expression, the same routine, the same body language, and the same "vibe," no matter what your hand is.

Inconsistency means something isn't quite right with the way a foe played his hand. For example, if there's Q-J-10 on board and he's representing A-K in the hole, why didn't he bet it preflop like he always has before? Inconsistencies in emotional message you grasp on an almost subliminal level. If you've ever seen someone smile without seeming happy (a phony smile), you get it. Somehow, a player's gestures don't seem to link up with the strong message inherent in the bet. Something seems weak. It's a lazy lie, a bluff by someone not comfortable with lying and who deep down doesn't want to do it. The internal turmoil, the unfamiliar ground, throws the *timing* of the bet off.

Clues in Card Handling

The attention (or lack thereof) a player lavishes on her cards can be very telling. What does she do when she first gets her hole cards? No matter how she hides it, there will be a reaction.

Is her heart racing? Or is she ready to fold? You cannot always see it, but you can usually feel it.

If you look left, some players in preflop Hold'em will be holding their two cards in their hand, ready to muck. What a great tell! More players you don't have to worry about. Still others, only slightly less obvious, remove their poker faces and don't try to disguise their imminent departure.

Watch Players Looking at Their Cards

Unless you're under the gun preflop, first watch the other players look at their hole cards. Don't peek at your own until you have to. Then look around before you commit yourself to the pot. Observe who's already decided to see the flop. Better players aren't obvious, but after they've taken that first peek, they always do something with the cards. It's common to pull them back toward their chips if it's a good hand. Placing some chips or a marker on top is a good indicator as well, because most players are too lazy to go through all that trouble if they are going to fold right away.

ASK JOHNNY QUADS

Should I watch the dealer put down the flop?

No. When the dealer is turning up the flop, don't watch the cards; watch players' *reactions* to the cards. You can look later. In Stud, watch for tells as players receive up cards.

Better players, however, sometimes will "play games" by putting the marker on there—then fold anyway. Or if they are in the blind, they use the marker to represent strength and discourage raises, so they can get in cheaply. But if it's a good hand, you can be sure the player will protect it somehow: wrap his hands around it, put chips on it, something, at least until others have ceased flipping their cards into the muck.

Avoid Looking at Hole Cards During a Hand

You shouldn't have to look at your hole cards. Memorize them. You don't necessarily have to recall suits, unless you're suited, but if you can't even remember your cards, you really have no business playing. If you have to return to your cards, it is a tell. It means you think you have something.

You can be sure your good opponents know their hole cards, so if you see one looking at or "analyzing" his hand, it is a move. He knows what he has. Now it's up to you to decide what he's up to. Watch for reaction whenever anyone goes back to his or her hand—it's a free second chance to pick up a tell.

CHAPTER 10

PLAY THE GAME: TEXAS HOLD'EM

Texas Hold'em has evolved from an obscure 1950s community-card variation called Hold Me Darling to the most popular poker game in the world. For most players, Hold'em is simply faster and more fun than other games, as well as more manageable financially. While you enter the hand holding only two cards, you get your next three after just one (small-bet) round. To see your sixth card it's just one more small bet.

High Cards and Kickers

Good Hold'em play is based on the simplest of principles: High cards beat low cards. Hold'em is a game of being in the lead and betting strongly, so you want that power in the hole. Hold'em is not a game to be chasing pair versus pair because if you improve, your opponent will often improve also, due to the community-card nature of the game. If you don't consistently start with higher cards than your foes, you will not win. So you don't want to be chasing with drawing hands like 8-7 unless you can get in cheaply and have a large field to pay you off should you hit. And as the hand progresses, you don't stay with the draw unless you're going for the nuts. In this case, you either have the pot odds to stay or have a reasonable chance at winning on a bluff when you miss. The good news is you will usually know if you are drawing at the nuts and can fold cheaply on the flop if you don't improve.

POKER POINTER

Community cards turn Hold'em into a controlled burn. For one thing, you usually know "where you are" in a hand. It is easier to predict opponents' holdings, you always know what the nut hand is, and hands are more competitive since 71 percent of your cards are shared with others. Because the hands are closer in value, the pots are bigger, and your player-reading skills become paramount.

But draws should be the exception. Unless you are in a "no fold'em Hold'em" game, in which almost everyone stays in, drawing hands are not the primary way to win at this game. You win by playing high cards with high kickers and, because you know so much about your opponents' hands, you use what they don't have against them.

Hand Domination

Besides the rare monster pocket pairs (aces, kings, queens), starting hands like A-K and A-Q have the power. You ask, "Aren't these drawing hands, since you don't even have a pair?" Well, they are not drawing hands in that they are the highest hand *right now*. Since it is 16-1 against someone being dealt a pocket pair, you figure your high ace is tops. Sure, in a ten-person game, *someone* will get a pair every other hand, but unless it is aces, kings, or queens, that pair just isn't that strong if it's not heads-up, because odds are there will be at least one overcard on the flop. And the chance of someone being dealt a pair of aces, kings, or queens is slim: about 73-1.

POKER POINTER

Don't mistake ring-game limit Hold'em with the no-limit game you see on television on the World Poker Tour or World Series of Poker. The no-limit game is not as much about cards as it is about betting, reading players, and guts. No-limit strategies are the opposite pole from the limit game discussed in this book.

Yes, you'll pair your hole card on the flop just three out of ten tries, but you can say the same about your opponents. Except for flopping "nothing," pairing a hole card is still the most frequent occurrence on the flop. All other results are freaks. If you hit, you know you have top pair with top kicker (with your ace-face hand). If you all miss, you're still high, and since you've bet preflop, you still control the hand. You can predict if your opponent has missed by knowing your players. The only bad result is if he pairs and you don't, and in that case you will likely have overcards. Unless your foe hits a longshot flop like two pair or trips or a straight-flush draw, other possibilities favor the high cards.

What you seek most with your high card/high kicker like A-J is for some sap to play A-8 or A-6 suited. This is called a dominated hand, and it is a big money loser. If you have A-K, the A-x has only three outs—pairing his "x" card (of which there are three remaining in the deck). With no improvement, your king kicker beats him, and an ace on board traps him. If the flop is A-9-5, he must pair his kicker to win—just a 12-percent shot with two cards to come—and even then you could pair your king. Being suited does not help. Two suited cards will make a flush just 6 percent of the time, and a third of those are runner-runner (made on the turn and the river). A dominated hand like A-x to A-K is a costly 3-to-1 dog from square one. Winning players avoid dominated hands.

There are exactly 1,326 possible starting hands in Hold'em. When you factor in the four suits, there are six ways of making a pair and sixteen ways of making any other hand. Since offsuit hands are the same, there are actually only 169 distinctly different hands: seventy-eight suited hands, seventy-eight unsuited hands, and thirteen pairs.

The top twenty moneymaking hands are generally considered to be aces, kings, queens, jacks, A-Ks, tens, A-K, A-Qs, K-Qs, A-Js, A-10s, A-Q, nines, K-Js, K-Q, K-10s, A-9s, A-J, eights, and Q-Js ("s" means suited).

Where Are the Aces?

Aces are your best friend in Hold'em, and you'll be dealt one 15 percent of the time (one out of seven hands). When you consider that your opponent has only a 6-percent chance of having a pocket pair, your ace seems even stronger. And even if someone does have a pair, you can still flop the *highest* pair. But be careful! You want your other friend guarding your back—a high kicker. Aces with low kickers are money-drainers. Realize that in a ten-handed game, if you have an ace, there is a 75-percent chance someone else out there has one, too. If you *don't* have an ace, there is an 84-percent chance of a bullet lurking out there. (In a five-handed game, if you have an ace, there is a 41-percent chance of someone else having one; if you don't, 51 percent of the time someone else will.) When an ace hits the board, you must take notice. And think about it. If an ace hits the flop, and you have an ace with a small kicker, can you call a bet?

POKER POINTER

With the exception of a pair of aces, any start hand in Hold'em can be folded preflop in the right situation. Examine the circumstances of the game before committing a penny to the pot, and always realize that a bad call early can cost you a lot more than just the preflop money.

The Importance of Starting Hands

Since second-best hands have a stubborn way of remaining second-best in Hold'em, your starting-hand selection is your most important decision. Knowing which hands to play—and not to play—is the difference between winning and losing, especially if you're new to the game.

A Hyper-aggressive Strategy

Some pros advise beginning players to raise and reraise strongly preflop with *all* pairs from aces down to sevens, as well as A-K and A-Q, in any position. The lack of positional consideration is a radical departure from most starting-hand strategies, and the emphasis is put on betting patterns and taking control. More skilled players can add the rest of the pocket pairs to their playable hands, as well as any suited ace and K-Q.

Under this philosophy, you can make it two bets to go with these additional hands, call if it's two bets to you, but fold for three bets. Advanced players can cautiously add suited connectors as low as 6-5 or 5-4 with enough callers. You will have to decide if this will work in your game.

Position and Hand Value
The more sensible (and prevailing) starting-hand strategies use position to determine a hand's worth. In early position, only hands that can stand a raise are played. As the button nears, more hands are added because there is less chance of a raise after you. Playable early-position hands are aces, kings, queens, and any A-K or A-Q. In middle position, pairs down through eights are added, as well as A-J, A-10, A-9, K-Q, K-J, K-10, Q-J, and Q-10 (suited or unsuited). Late position adds the rest of the pairs, all suited aces, K-9, Q-9, J-10, and suited connectors down through 9-8.

A more conservative philosophy gives some value to suited starting hands and advocates only playing pairs aces through jacks and A-K suited in early position. Tens, any A-K, and A-Q, A-J, and K-Q (all suited) are added as position improves, then nines, any A-Q, and J-10, Q-J, K-J, and A-10 (all suited). The remaining pairs, suited aces, suited connectors, and face-face offsuit hands can be added as you near the button, depending on game conditions and whether you can get in cheaply.

In Hold'em, to win, you must beat all the other hands. You need more than the best hand—you must have the best hand against all the other hands combined. This is the main reason it is almost always right to thin the field with the lead, and it's also why more players in the hand diminishes the value of pairs and increases the value of drawing hands.

Nothing Is Written in Stone

Unfortunately, there is no hard-and-fast list of starting hands that will make this crucial decision easy. In their well-known book *Hold'em Poker for Advanced Players,* which favors a strict positional concept, authors David Sklansky and Mason Malmuth point out that "Starting hands actually move up and down the hand rankings depending on the circumstance. Because of this, it can be a mistake to rigidly adhere to the hand rankings."

Good players adjust their starting hand play based not just on position but also on whether a pot has been raised and if the game is loose or tight, aggressive (much raising) or passive (little raising). So starting hand "rankings" should be only a guide. That said, let's look at starting hands in detail. (In the following discussions, a loose game means many players seeing the flop. A tight game means few seeing the flop. As always, strategies should be tempered by your table image.)

Which Hands Are Playable?

There are two types of playable hands: powerful high hands that can win without improvement against a small field, and speculative drawing hands (like medium-suited connectors) that cry out for a larger field to get that big payday when they finally hit. Position will control whether you fold, call, or raise with most hands, drawing hands especially. Your lower pairs and connectors just cannot be played in early position because you do not know the size of the field, and most aren't worth calling a raise with. If you don't believe that, try limping in with pocket fives or 8-7 and then note your reaction when you are raised and are left facing one or two players, both of whom have better hands than you. You need a miracle flop, and you won't win much if you get it.

Playing High Pocket Pairs

Pocket aces are the best of the best. You are a huge favorite over any other single hand, and there is no chance of an overcard on the flop. Your objectives are to maximize your profit and keep others from drawing out on you. A fine line this is indeed, since to make money you must have callers, but callers increase your risk. This is the line you must find in every hand you play. Do you want callers here? Yes. Do you want the whole table to call? No, too many odd things can happen. With aces, your preflop strategy focuses on getting two or three callers—no more than four, where you could be an underdog to the field.

If you're in early position in a loose game, call, but reraise if you get the chance. If it's super-loose, raise right away because you'll get callers. In middle position, raise if there is at least one caller before you. Reraise if someone behind you raises. In late position, raise if you have at least one caller. Call if it's just you and the blinds.

If you're in early position in a tight game, call, but reraise if you are raised. In middle position, raise if you have a caller before you, and call if you have a raiser before you. In late position, raise if you have two or more callers or raisers in front of you, otherwise call. Don't get married to aces. While you never lay down pocket rockets preflop, later, if it's clear you are beat, fold 'em.

Pocket Kings

The Number Two hand is almost as powerful as aces. If you don't flop a set, you'll still face an ace on the flop only once every eight hands; so you can play kings like you do aces, except a little more strongly, because you don't want to let in drawing hands with aces, like A-x suited or an ace with a card five-or-under that would've folded for a raise. If hands with that dreaded ace are going to play, at least make them pay. You can be a little coy with kings in a tight game, but don't pull this move as often as with aces. Aces are really the only hand in lower-limit games where you can argue for a frequent slow-play. Kings and aces are the only (non-drawing) hands where you can be thinking about maximizing profit preflop, rather than aggressively thinning the field.

Pocket Queens

A pair of ladies is the cutoff hand between thinking you have the pot already won and being nervous. You will face an overcard without a set one out of three hands. With aces and kings as your only overcards, you're in trouble when one hits, as these are the most likely cards your foes will play. So raise as early and as often as you can with queens.

POKER POINTER

A straight-flush draw in Hold'em has fifteen outs, giving you a 54-percent chance of hitting a straight, flush, or straight flush with two cards to come. If you have two overcards that could win for you, that's six more outs! This is one of the few times when a draw could actually be favored to win.

The only time you wouldn't is if you feel like gambling a bit, or if you're on the button with no callers and want to let the blinds in cheap, hoping for a flop like J-9-6 when one of them has a jack or nine. Generally, queens do not want a large field.

Playing Medium and Low Pairs

Medium pairs are jacks through sevens. Though jacks may seem a lot stronger than sevens, they are really in the same boat. They may be the best hand preflop, but odds are they will face at least one overcard. These are the hands you would love to play heads-up or go all-in with in no-limit—after all, there are only three higher preflop hands than jacks—but in lower-limit they will tie your stomach up in knots.

In some games, you can play jacks and tens the same as queens, raising like mad, then betting on the flop and hoping everyone folds. With nines, eights, and sevens you can raise (or reraise) early to thin the field in a tight game, but if you already have callers in front of you, your best course is to just call, since it's obvious many will see the flop, where you will certainly face the dreaded overcard. These hands are not strong against a large field, unless a rare flop of all low cards hits. These five hands are also difficult to play in an aggressive game from early or middle position, since you don't want to be calling a lot of raises. Remember, you'll only make a set 12 percent of the time. The general rule for these hands goes as follows: Jam in a tight game, limp in a loose game. Multiple flop overcards mean fold.

Lower Pairs

Pairs sixes and below in limit Hold'em are generally played for their set value. That is, if you don't flop a set, you're out of the hand. Since you're trying to get in cheap, you can't play them in early position because they are not worth a raise, and they are only worthwhile in middle position in a loose-passive game. If you're more aggressive, you can raise near the button if there's just a caller or two. You'll get the blinds out and win the pot on the flop if no one else hits. Only in the tightest games should you raise with these hands in early or middle position if you're first in, the idea being to get it heads-up, sow confusion, or buy the blinds. In most games, your philosophy should be to treat them as drawing hands: Limp in late with a large field and pray for a set or the high end of an open-end straight draw.

Fearing the Flop with Low and Medium Pairs

What are the chances that you will *dislike* the flop if you have a pocket pair? In other words, that you will not flop a set, and there will be at least one overcard on the flop? Here they are: kings, 12 percent; queens, 31 percent; jacks, 47 percent; tens, 60 percent; nines, 69 percent; eights, 77 percent; sevens, 82 percent; sixes, 85 percent; fives, 87 percent; fours, 88 percent; threes, 88 percent; and twos, 88 percent.

There's a reason the overcard is such a killer for lower pairs. If you are facing a higher pair, you usually have only two outs (the other two cards of the same value as your pair, to make trips). (If you have two overcards against a pair, you have six outs.) Compare the overcard to your opponents. Ask yourself, "Would they have played a hand with a nine?" The problem with the lower pairs is that you have to fold to most raises, even if you might still have the best hand.

The Power Hands

A-K and A-Q (suited or unsuited) are hands you can raise and reraise with in any position. They are not meant to be slow-played, as you do not yet have a made hand. A-K need fear no hand except aces and kings. A-Q need fear no hand except pocket aces, kings, queens, and A-K. In a heads-up game, these hands are a coin-flip to win against any lower pair, but in actual play—when played aggressively—they blow away low and medium pairs. Those pairs have trouble calling both before and after the flop because the pair always has to be concerned with facing a higher pocket pair and, of course, flopped overcards.

Ace with Face Card

A-K and A-Q can be played the same. If you have A-Q, you should not worry that the person with the other preflop ace has a king kicker—it's just too rare. These are hands you play for their high-card value. If you pair on the flop, it's a cinch that you will have top pair and top kicker, which is your goal. You also sometimes have a straight possibility. The good news is it will be the nut straight. The bad news is it will always be an inside straight. But you don't play these hands for their straight value, and, if your cards are suited, you are not playing for the flush. You do not make flushes often enough for that even to enter your thinking. You play these hands the same suited or unsuited.

With A-K and A-Q, jam it preflop, and bet out again with most flops even if you miss. Maybe you can buy one. A-J is strong, but it's less powerful than A-K and A-Q. How aggressively you play it will depend on your personality and the game. A-10 is a borderline hand that can only be played strong in late position (or middle position if you're first in). There's a 75-percent chance that someone else has an ace, and if he or she has a higher kicker, you're a 3-to-1 dog. A-J and A-10 are hands that should be folded if there is a lot of raising.

Other Hands with an Ace

With A-x suited (any suited ace with a kicker below ten), your objective depends on the game, but remember: This is a drawing hand, not an ace (power) hand! In a loose game, you always play these hands, but get in as cheaply as possible because you'll only make a flush 4 percent of the time (not counting runner-runner). In a tight game, you fold in early position, and limp in middle position (fold to a raise). But sometimes you will raise in late position, setting up a bluff later into a small field after a ragged flop. You're looking for a four-flush, two pair, or to pair your "x" card on the flop. Pairing your ace might only make you second best. The small field in tight games makes your flush draws less attractive, so you only enter unraised pots. Generally, treat A-x suited as a speculative hand that needs a limp-in or large field to be playable. This is true unless you're in a weak game, where you can go in ramming and jamming and buy pots on the flop or turn even if you miss.

Unsuited aces with kickers nine or lower are trap hands. Only play them in late position with few callers in front of you or in unraised pots, short-handed games, or to steal the blinds.

Suited Connectors—and More

High suited connectors K-Q, Q-J, and J-10 are tease hands. They look so good, but they don't always deliver. K-Q is a bona fide hand you can raise with in any position, but the other two are not as strong because if you just hit a pair, you could have kicker trouble. Your best bet is a straight draw, because the flush draw will not be to the nuts. With J-10, you can make an open-end straight draw three ways, and you can make the nut straight five ways. That said, with Q-J and J-10, you still want to see the flop as cheaply as possible, so against good players you must fold them in early position. Just limp in a loose game if you're in middle and late position, but raise in a tight game if you're first or second in.

Suited connectors below J-10 look pretty, but they are longshots, and they are weak since pairing a hole card usually doesn't help you. These are drawing hands looking for a cheap entry into a large field, so only play them in later position, when you are sure you won't be raised, or in "family pots." Don't ever play below 5-4 suited.

Unsuited Connectors

Besides A-K, K-Q is the only premium unsuited connector. It can be played from any position, but think hard before raising with it early. Q-J, J-10, and 10-9 are playable in middle or late position depending on the game, though not for more than one raise. High unsuited one-gap hands—K-J, Q-10, and J-9—are also playable late. Lower unsuited connectors and one-gappers are strictly for the button, "family pots," and in the blinds when you want to gamble.

Suited Kings

With suited kings, you are entering the realm of the loose players. These hands are money-losers, but for those who like to see flops, they are a good excuse. K-J and K-10 are okay middle-position hands, suited or unsuited, and if you raise, it won't be on the merit of the hand but for strategic purposes. You can limp late with any K-x suited only into a large field with no raises. Unsuited, don't play less than K-10 or perhaps K-9.

Fold Other Hands

Other hands are trash, and you save big money by folding them. This includes the classic loser hand: any two suited cards. With the exception of limping with A-x and K-x (x is nine or below) into a large field, never play a hand just because it is suited. Unless a hand has been discussed above, just muck it! Be wary when playing the top and bottom end of a straight, as with K-9. If the board has Q-J-10, you will be killed by A-K—often. "Gap" hands like 10-8 and 8-6 are over-rated. There is less chance of an open-end draw than with the connectors, and fewer of your draws will be to the nuts. Being able to fold hands in Hold'em is a big part of your edge. Better players play fewer hands.

POKER POINTER

There are many different philosophies on playing the blinds. Most low-limiters will always throw in the other half bet in the small blind, and automatically call one raise in the big blind. Better players don't throw in a cent if the hand doesn't deserve it. One thing is certain: If the flop is ragged, watch out for the blinds. With their random hands, they might have hit something!

The All-Important Flop

The flop is the critical juncture of the hand. You have two calculations on the flop, and they must be made quickly—without staring at the board. The first is whether the flop helped you. The second is whether it helped one or more of your opponents. The good news is you will know the first, and you can predict the second by knowing the kind of cards your foes play in certain positions (and for how many bets), and remembering the wagering prior to the flop.

In return for boosting the pot, preflop bettors and raisers have given something up—anonymity. Hold'em is a funny game. Some players won't reraise with anything but pocket aces, while others love to build pots. Good players don't call preflop raises without a serious hand unless they are playing against total maniacs, in which case they *still* make sure they have something. Generally, it takes a better hand to call a bet than it does to make the initial wager. (Since the preflop aggressor—last raiser—controls the hand, you should almost always bet on the flop if you've raised preflop, even with nothing. If everyone has missed, you pick up the pot.) Thus, a bet from a preflop raiser might not mean anything, but bets from others do.

POKER POINTER

If the flop has missed you, it's probably hit someone else if you have multiple opponents, unless it's total rags. The more players seeing the flop, the more luck is involved in winning the hand, and the less skill.

When the flop comes, you can compare it to what you think the preflop aggressors were betting on. If a ragged flop like 8-6-3 shows up, for a preflop bettor to now have a real hand, he or she would have to have started with a high pocket pair, a rare holding. Two pair is out of the question and you can't live in fear of sets, so an ace-face hand is much more probable. Ask yourself, "What hands would the preflop aggressor raise on?" If your foe only raises on powerhouses, you're now better off with a drawing hand if you have the odds to call than to go up against A-K or A-Q with your A-10. You can get away from drawing hands like Q-J, J-10, or A-x suited on the flop if they don't pan out—a quick exit is part of their value.

Your hand is only as good as the flop that goes with it. Even aces can be crushed by the wrong three cards. No matter how good your hole cards, they can be folded if there is a troublesome flop. The most common problem is overcards, whose presence often means you are facing a higher pair. The more opponents you're playing against, the more probable that pair.

If you think someone has a higher pair than you on the flop, you are cooked unless you have the pot odds to play a four-flush, open-end straight, or gutshot (inside) straight with a hole card paired. All of these you'll make one out of three tries. But look at the depressing probability of improving your inferior hand by the river when you face an overpair. If you have a pocket pair, chance is 8 percent; two overcards, 24 percent; one overcard, 13 percent; one hole card paired, 20 percent; and with two undercards, forget it.

So Many Flops, So Little Time

With more than 19,000 possible flops, it is impossible to discuss them all, but there are general patterns. Remember, the fewer the players, the more chance the flop has missed them. The more players, the more chance someone has hit. Be aware that the flop will only hit the typical hand one out of three times (not counting straight and flush draws). But if you include draws, high suited overcard hands like A-K and A-10 will hit the flop a whopping 52 percent of the time!

Unlike Stud with its commonplace two pair and trips, Hold'em is often won by a hand with just top pair on the board—that is, the flop is K-10-7 and you have a king in the hole with a high, bettable kicker (queen or ace, maybe jack). This is your bread-and-butter hand and you must bet it strong, so you cannot fear the worst-case scenarios on every flop. Flopping two pair, trips, and four-flushes are aberrations. Don't worry about aberrations in poker unless someone tells you in no uncertain terms that he has one.

Having top pair doesn't mean you are a shoo-in. Watch the board for combinations with cards that a lot of people play—like a bundle of cards ten and above. If you have multiple opponents, your high pair could be in trouble. Protect your hand aggressively here. If you are facing flush and/or straight draws on the flop, do everything you can to get them out. Don't give free cards: Make them call multiple bets, or fold. If you have top pair and top kicker and are raised, you're going to stay for the turn unless there's a raising war going on. After the turn, with the big bets coming, you will be forced to evaluate whether your top pair is worth taking to the river. If you are only called on the flop, you bet your top pair on the turn no matter what card comes off, even if it's an overcard.

POKER POINTER

Decide early what your objective is with your hand. Is it a power hand, or a draw, or a prayer? Does it call for a large field, small field, or heads-up? Are you going to play as cheaply as possible, or push the action? Don't play a hand without a plan!

Take notice of what kind of cards your opponents are playing. This is everything on the flop. In some games, no one will play a hand with a card below ten. Others won't play a card below six, except with an ace, while others only will

The following are the odds of making a hand after the flop. All Hold'em players should know this chart. Note: The percentages are rounded up.

Outs	2 cards to go	1 card to go	Comment
20	68%	44%	
19	65%	41%	
18	62%	39%	Open-straight-flush draw with 1 overcard
17	60%	37%	
16	57%	35%	
15	54%	33%	Straight-flush draw open-ended
14	51%	30%	Still better than 50-50
13	48%	28%	Open-ender with a pair
12	45%	26%	Four-flush with winning overcard
11	42%	24%	Four-straight with winning overcard
10	38%	22%	Flopped set, no full house on turn
9	35%	20%	Four-flush on the flop
8	32%	17%	Four-straight, open-ended
7	28%	15%	Inside straight with winning overcard
6	24%	13%	Need to pair either hole card
5	20%	11%	Paired a hole card, need to hit kicker
4	17%	9%	Inside straight; both hole cards paired
3	13%	7%	Need to pair a specific hole card
2	8%	4%	Pocket pair; need a set
1	4%	2%	Need a single specific card in the deck

play six or under with a suited ace. In other games folks will play any suited or connected cards. You must consider this when evaluating every flop. Now is the time to put players on hands using their tendencies, the preflop bet pattern, the flop, and the flop bets.

Strategy and Tactics on the Flop

Much of your flop strategy is predicated on your having bet, raised, or reraised before the flop and taken control of the hand. Unless you are considered wild and loose, a preflop bet can be essential to winning post-flop. As has been stressed throughout this book, it is critical to be in a game where players will fold hands and where you can reduce the number of opponents. In limit, sometimes you are "limited" as to how much monetary pressure you can exert because there are only so many bets, and the amount of the bet is "limited." Still, it can be done, and it starts preflop. If you are going in, go in raising. If you are playing a drawing hand like A-x suited, suited connectors, or a medium or low pair, you have two choices. You can limp in and fold if you don't hit the flop, or you can raise and then bet the flop strongly whether you hit or not. This latter strategy is very effective against the right players, and if you don't buy the pot, at least you have sent out a "feeler" and know if you are beat.

You Flop Nothing

Welcome to the club! You have nothing, but what of the others? Will they fold to a bet? Did you bet preflop? If so, maybe they're ready to muck. If the flop is ragged, your high ace might still be high. Bet it.

POKER POINTER

When playing a draw such as a four-straight, four-flush, small pair with overcard kicker, or pair with a gutshot in late position, raise the bettor on the flop. On the next round, the field will often check to you, and you can then check as well, thus getting a free card on the more expensive turn. An alternative play on the turn is to bet like you've got something. Since the others have now shown weakness, you might buy the pot there or on the river.

You Flop Top Pair

If the pair is high, you bet if you have a high kicker. If you have a *low* kicker, well, why are you in the hand? You'll just have to bet—and pray. If the pair is medium or small, like if you have 8-7 and the flop is 8-4-2, you still bet, because you figure no one else has played the low cards. If you're in a loose game where everyone is seeing the flop, then you check, as someone likely has K-8, J-8, or something similar. If you face a raise and reraise, you might have to dump your hand as you may have two pair and/or a set against you. Beware of players who will bump it on just a draw.

You Flop Second or Third Pair

How high is the flop? There is a big difference between having third pair if the flop is A-K-J and if it is 8-6-5. Are your adversaries likely to have the higher pair? The smaller the field and the more ragged the flop, the more valuable second and third pair become. If you sense weakness, bet if you think you are the only one with a pair. This strategy makes you about a 3-1 favorite against two overcards. Knowing when to play second or third pair is one of the advanced skills in Hold'em that come only with time, and yes, second pair *is* better than third pair.

You Flop a Good Draw

If you have four to a high flush on the flop, or an open-end straight (the high end!), and two or more opponents (more is better), you will almost always have the pot odds to take the hand to the river. But you have some decisions. If you face a large field, one philosophy is to get in as cheaply as possible. After all, you'll only hit the hand one out of three tries, and bluffing will be difficult if you miss. On the other hand, with many opponents, you may want to build the pot if you're drawing at the nuts. Well, here's some food for thought. You're a 4-1 dog to hit your four-flush or open straight on the turn, but if you have five people calling, you make a "profit" on every bet.

POKER POINTER

All flops that do not include a pair or trips will have a straight draw except for K-8-3, K-8-2, K-7-2, and Q-7-2.

Against a small field, semi-bluff if you think your one, two, or three foes are capable of tossing their hands later. If you miss on the turn, you'll make your hand on the river only one out of five tries, but the semi-bluff gives you another way out. Any draw with fourteen or more outs, such as a nut flush draw with a pair or a straight-flush draw, should always be bet and raised strongly.

You Have a Longshot Draw

If your chances are slim but you have proper odds from the pot (and you can afford it), go for it! Inside straights are 5-1 with two cards to come and 10-1 on the river, while hitting runner-runner flush is 23-1 and unplayable. You only have two cards in the deck to make a set with your pocket pair, and three outs to pair your pocket ace, so fold these hands. There is one draw that is often overlooked: the pair with an inside straight. You have nine outs here, the same as with a four-flush. One note of caution: If you hit your inside straight, it often is *not* the nuts.

You Flop a Freak Hand

These are two pair, trips, straights, flushes, and higher. This is where experience comes in. You're obviously tops right now—and have already won the hand in most cases— so evaluate the chance of someone drawing out on you. The greater the chance, the more you should bet. With two pair and trips, you usually will bet and raise, as well as with the low end of straights and low flushes. With higher hands, you let them catch up a bit. If you're in a game where everyone calls and no one believes you, then of course you bet, bet, bet! If you're in a tight game, be more conservative. Be guided by how obvious your hand is. A flush is obvious, while a straight is usually much less so.

Playing on the Turn

In lower-limit games, many players will call a single "small" flop bet with marginal hands, but they will give it up when faced with a big bet on the turn. This is a turning point—the time of maximum financial pressure, where many pots are there for the taking. But many who bluff or semi-bluff on the flop will make the mistake of checking the turn, thinking that those who called on the flop have real hands. In fact, they frequently do not. They just didn't care as much about the small flop bet and would've folded on the turn if someone just kept the pressure on. Bet into weakness on the turn, but notice if someone's draw could've gotten there, such as when a third flush card hits. Don't fear the flush automatically, unless you have put someone on a flush draw before the turn. The more opponents, of course, the greater the chance someone has it.

You don't fear a third straight card as much as a third flush card on the turn, but the scariest card of all is a third high card. Since so many low-limit denizens play any two cards ten or above, a third high one threatens two pair or a straight or just plain trouble.

Other turn-card observations:

- If you have seen the turn on a draw, you usually will have the pot odds to see the river as well, provided you are not facing two bets or more. For two or more big bets with only one card to come, make sure the pot is big enough to take a stab at. You're more than a 4-1 dog with most draws at this point.
- If you bet preflop and on the flop, but you check the turn, they will put you on A-K or A-Q, or sometimes a flush draw if there was one on the flop. (A-K can sometimes win without improvement.)
- If you've made up your mind to call on the river, why not raise on the turn? It frequently won't cost you any

more and gives you control of the hand. Then, on the river, you can bluff or get a free call.

- It can be scary if the board pairs on the turn. Here is where it really helps you to have put players on a hand. Is it plausible—given the betting pattern preflop and on the flop and knowing the players—for someone to have trips now?

Overall, the turn is a good time to fold, but it's also a time to use the higher limits to make your adversaries squirm.

Playing on the River

The river: This is where the hopes and dreams of you and your fellow card-holding human beings come crashing down in ruins or join together like a successful space shuttle launch. And no one can tell you, except in the most general of terms, how to play here.

The Street of Dreams

In many ways, the river is the easiest street to play. You know your final hand, and if you are a solid player, you have a good idea of what others are holding. You know the flop, how the betting has gone, what the nut hand is. You know how much it will cost you.

If your only way of winning is a bluff, decide whether it has a chance. Don't waste your money if it doesn't, but don't be shy, either. In a weak pot, the first bettor often takes it. Judgment and experience come into play here. If you feel the odds against your bluff working are 5-1, but the pot is offering you 7-1, then it's worth a shot. And if you think someone might bluff you, say, one out of six times, but the pot is giving you 9-1, well, you should call.

The questions you ask on the river are pretty fundamental, but the answers are based on all the information you have collected during the hand. You should know the answers to questions like these: Do you have the best hand? Should you bluff? Are you being bluffed? Did anyone improve on the river?

If you've absorbed what's gone before in this book and gone out and played, you will have some internal stars to guide you. But there is one certainty here: The river is no time to back off. Don't miss river bets! If there is a good chance you are best, make them pay.

Fearing River Cards

If you've been putting your opponents on hands, you know what cards you *don't* want to see on the river. You know the cards that will beat you. Don't just automatically give up if you miss. Everyone else may be in the same boat.

While aces always get your attention, you shouldn't panic over hands that are made on *both* turn and river. Most people don't hang around for runner-runner unless they are allowed to limp in on the flop. Were there flop bets? How many? Any bets preflop? You don't fear runner-runner suited cards (as in J♣-Q♥-7♠-6♣-3♣), a turn-river pair (J♣-Q♥-7♠-6♦-6♣), or two cards that make a three-card sequence on the board (J♣-Q♥-6♠-5♦-4♠). More scary than these late-developing hands are cards that would fit in with something a player could have been playing on the flop, such as a four-flush (J♣-Q♥-7♥-K♦-6♥).

ASK JOHNNY QUADS

Should a turn-river pair ever scare me?

Yes, if it's a high card and someone bet it up on the turn, or if you have paired both hole cards and they are low—for example, you have 8-7 and the flop is A-8-7, with the turn and river 2-2. Anyone with an ace (or pocket pair above eight) now beats you.

Buying Pots at the Eleventh Hour

Stealing pots on the river when you've missed your hand is a dicey thing. If everyone has checked to you, you have to bet. If you're first and a blank hits the river, you might buy the pot by being first in. The more opponents (and the larger the pot), the harder this task is. The higher the limit, the easier it is. If the river card is a blank, the pot usually goes to the player in control. If no one's in control, evaluate your odds of a successful bluff. If the river is a good card—like a third flush card, ace, or high scare card—you can bluff if you sense weakness. It won't always work, but it doesn't have to work every time to be a moneymaker. While fancy plays like slow-playing, check-raising, and bluffing should be the exception rather than the rule, sometimes a river bluff is the only way you can win.

Keep the ancient proverb close to your heart: "Though I walk through the valley of the shadow of death, I will fear no river." Or that other saying of the grizzled old gamblers: "On the river, your odds are 50-50—either he's got it, or he don't!"

CHAPTER 11

ONLINE AND TOURNAMENT POKER

Over the past few years, two phenomena have combined to push poker into the stratosphere and into your living room: Internet casinos and tournament poker. Can't find a game? Too tired to leave the house? Online cardrooms can have you in action at the click of a mouse. And if you're looking for the most extreme, cutting-edge brand of poker, the tournament table may be right up your alley.

The Double-Edged Sword of Internet Poker

At first glance, the Internet seems like a godsend for pressed-for-time or isolated poker aficionados. Of course, when it comes to gambling, when something seems too good to be true, it usually is.

Advantages of Online Casinos

Look at this formidable "plus" column. You can always find a game—without driving, or trying to organize your friends. If you just have an hour or two, you can jump on your computer and be in action in minutes. If you are home-bound, you can still play—with limits as low as a quarter. If the brick-and-mortar casinos won't deal your favorite game, some online rooms will. Most sites have a large variety of games and limits, day or night—including tournaments. Changing tables is a snap, there's no smoke, and you can even play in multiple games at the same time—in your underwear!

POKER POINTER

Online poker is good for learning the basics. Most Web sites offer no-risk "play money" games for free, and in real-money games, you and a few pals can gather around the computer and discuss your hand before you act.

Those who struggle in face-to-face games love playing online. No one can discover their tells, and strangers and superior players can't intimidate them. Those who play unorthodox poker or who find the casino crowd too critical feel right at home online. It's also much easier to be aggressive without tough players staring you down. Some people just like to be anonymous—and you don't have to tip the dealer! Besides not having to tip, some sites sweeten the financial pot by offering free tournaments ("freerolls") for those who have played enough hands, bad-beat jackpots, and deposit bonuses. The rake is usually less as well.

You're Not in Kansas Anymore

Not all the differences between online and brick-and-mortar games are good ones. For the undisciplined, the lure of a poker game in the next room of your house can be too much. The play is so fast—sixty or more hands per hour—that it becomes mesmerizing. The rake, blinds, and antes can eat you up quickly. Sitting at the computer, it's so easy to keep seeing hand after hand. It's tempting to play loose, to just click that mouse and call, card after card, or suddenly bluff off a lot of chips on a whim. In a casino, a bluff is a major move. Online, you just click the mouse and off go the chips.

Money management can go up in cybersmoke along with discipline. After awhile, the chips don't seem real—until you get your credit-card bill. It is way too simple to waste time and money online. Playing multiple games is foolish, and players who say they can do it effectively are kidding themselves. All they are doing is being raked and blinded twice as fast. And don't forget the very real problem of "mis-clicking"—hitting the "raise" or "call" button when you meant to hit "fold." That happens more than players will admit.

Online Strategy Changes

Since so much of good poker is "playing the player, not playing the cards," you can see how Internet games could be a nightmare. Forget finding tells, discovering someone's personality, reading body language, betting motions, or any of the other myriad mannerisms that provide information to the astute player. You won't see through opponents' tricky moves, and making moves of your own will be difficult.

However, strategy isn't totally nonexistent. Following are a few pointers.

Find a Promising Table

This is much easier online because you can observe any table you wish for as long as you wish. You can take notes, get a feel for the players, and determine if the crowd's loose or tight. The sites even help you out. The games will be listed in their "lobbies," along with the number of seated players, waiting list, average pot size, and percentage of players seeing the flop (or fourth street in Stud).

Screen-Name Misdirection

Controlling your table image and using deception is problematic, but you can make a stab it at with your betting patterns and with your screen name. Using betting to manipulate isn't as effective online, so for the most part it's best to play in a straightforward manner. Acting real loose for a while so you can act tight later (or vice versa) is futile when you don't know if anyone is even paying attention and players change tables so often.

Over time, if you play with the same characters for hours on end, you might get a line on someone. This is where you can exercise a big cyberadvantage: taking notes! You can scribble like a banshee, unlike in a casino, where you would be considered a nutcase. Some sites even provide a screen area to take notes on. (Your note-taking will not be in vain because most sites will not allow players to change their screen names once they are established. Their only recourse is to close the account or to open multiple accounts.)

Your screen name, your state or country, and the figure you choose to represent you (on some sites) provide the bulk of your table image. They reveal valuable information (and misinformation!), so make sure you are delivering the impression you want others to see—usually a misleading one. Likewise, watch for deliberately misleading screen names and icons (also called "avatars") and for those who are playing it straight.

POKER POINTER

If you decide to play online, your chosen site will walk you through all the details of funding your account, and so on. But before you begin real-money play, go to the "play money" tables and practice using the software (the various buttons) so you can concentrate on the game and avoid costly mistakes when you finally dive in.

"Chatting" Can Reveal a Lot

There is also a "chat" area where you can type messages to other players during the game. Often, this is where you will experience one of the negative aspects of cyberspace: anonymous cowards typing sarcastic insults and sexual innuendoes.

Still, chatting can yield some valuable info. Like real-world conversation, you can sometimes get someone on your side, discover his or her personality and age, or get a line on how someone plays, how many games he or she is playing in, and how long your opponent has been at the table. Up all night? On tilt? And it never hurts to play dumb and ask for advice. It might not be right, but it will be revealing!

Pot Odds Become Huge Online

Although reading players is more difficult, you can still utilize your loose and tight game strategies and especially position play and pot odds. Pot odds calculations grow in value as your other skills lessen. A pot is a pot—online or not. Good position is good position. Play your quality starting hands, don't play too long, and let the pot be your guide. And if you think it will be less humiliating to go broke alone at home than in a casino, you might be in for a rude awakening.

Are There Tells Online?

Many online players insist that finding tells, noticing body language, table image, and "playing the player" is over-rated. They say tells can be manipulated and that you can learn more by just following the money—that is, by studying the pattern of bets, checks, raises, and calls during a hand. But you can study the betting in brick-and-mortar rooms as well, along with everything else. And players can use their betting patterns to mislead, just as with false tells.

Some online players believe that the speed at which players click their call, bet, or raise buttons can be a tell. You can discover some moves if you play with the same players long enough. For example, if someone hesitates and then checks, that means weak (the player wanted you to think he was considering a bet). If a player has clicked the automatic "check" or "check/fold" button, the decision will show up as an instantaneous action on your screen when it is his or her turn. This is revealing. You know he was ready to fold. On the other hand, when someone hits the bet or raise button quickly, does that mean a bluff, or does it indicate a strong hand? This is where your notes come in handy.

Don't Be a Sucker!

The Internet is rampant with stories from players who feel they've been taken, either by opponents in collusion, the sites themselves, or both. There is no question that it happens. What is unknown is how prevalent it is. And since these sites are poorly regulated, who are you going to complain to?

"Active" Collusion Between Players

This isn't much different than in a casino where two players "whipsaw" an unsuspecting rube with raise after raise, but the trick is much more effective online. Here, the cheaters can discuss their hands by cell phone or even play on different computers in the same room! In a casino, this scam can get obvious, but online, where you can't look players in the eye, you're left wondering. Some sites have installed software to detect collusion, and the word is out that they are being diligent about it, but it's small consolation complaining to a site after you've been bet out of pot after pot or whipsawed into oblivion.

This type of collusion is certainly easier and more effective online, but because of the computer record of hands, it is also easier to detect—after the fact. On the other hand, cyber play is so fast that by the time you realize what happened, many hands may have gone by.

"Passive" Collusion Between Players

This brand of cheating is subtler and harder to catch. Again, a number of players get an edge by sharing their cards—obviously a major advantage when figuring odds and deciding which starting hands to play. This might not sound like much, but to a gambler, a small edge makes a big difference. Wouldn't you like to know what three of your opponents are holding?

Hackers

If a teenager can hack into the Pentagon, someone should be able to hack into a poker site, right? The sites say that their encryption software is as sophisticated as that of any online bank, and that only your computer is given information on your hole cards. So no nefarious nerd will be able to read your hidden hand by hacking a Web site. But ask yourself this: How safe is your home computer?

"All-in" Scamming

This is probably the most common abuse of the Internet system and has caused much controversy in the poker world. In the early days, when faced with a tough decision, some unethical players were just refusing to act, and thus were "timed out." A "timed out" player was treated as if he went "all-in" (ran out of chips) at the point he failed to act, the same as if his computer crashed or his service provider had a glitch and disconnected the player from the Internet. Remaining players built a side pot.

Today, most sites will "fold" the hand of anyone not acting. However, a player who disconnects himself from the Internet will still be put all-in, so the scam survives, but many cyber rooms *are* cracking down. Players suspecting abuse can e-mail site administrators, who can review the hand in question and other hands played by the perpetrator, looking for a pattern. In cases of abuse, they may bar the client from the site or even confiscate his chips and transfer them to victims.

POKER POINTER

If your Internet connection is legitimately lost during a hand, you will still be put all-in (treated as if you've run out of chips), as long as you haven't used up your ration of "all-ins" for that day. Find out your site's policy on all-in protection before you play.

Cheating by Sites?

You may comfort yourself with the logical argument that Internet casino owners are making enough money *without* cheating. While this may be true, some still do it anyway. In fact, the really ruthless ones consider it a point of honor not to let a "sucker" get away with any of "their" money—or any money at all. The bottom line: If you are going to play online, you have to go in with both eyes open.

What Is a Tournament?

A tournament is an adrenaline-fueled competition using a fixed buy-in paid by anywhere from ten to over a thousand players. With the exception of the early stages of some "rebuy" events, you can't purchase more chips, so if you lose them all, you go home. Blinds and antes increase at regular intervals, ratcheting up the pressure. The tournament ends when one player (the winner) owns every chip.

Competing in a tournament is intense. The chance to play for prizes in the thousands or even millions of dollars against the best players in the world is intoxicating, especially because your losses are limited to your buy-in. On a smaller scale, you can have a blast in $25 or $50 buy-in events where you may have hours of fun for very little money. You can also try your hand at small buy-in "satellite" events, where the winner receives an entry into a major tournament. And satellites aren't only at tournament venues. They are also all over the Internet.

ASK JOHNNY QUADS

What are the four main factors controlling whether you play a particular hand in a tournament?

Consider how many chips you have relative to others at your table, strength of the hand, position, and opponents (who they are and whether they have already called).

But before you quit your day job and hit the tournament trail, realize that not only will you be facing serious professionals, but many of them play hundreds of tournaments a year—and still can go months without reaching a final table. You can play extremely well in a tournament and yet come up empty, because usually only the final 10 percent win money.

It's About Survival

If you decide to tackle tournaments, you can leave your ring-game strategy at home. Of course, you still use your skills. You still read opponents and put them on hands, but tournaments require a new way of thinking. Since you can't dig into your pocket for more cash, you must never lose all your chips. It follows that if you are ever going to risk your last chips, not only do you want the best of it, you want very much the best of it—especially if you are one of the better players. If possible, you don't want to risk elimination if there's a significant chance of an unpleasant "surprise." You have three goals, and you take them one at a time:

1. **To finish in the money.** You want some payoff for all that hard work.
2. **To place in the top three.** This is where the really big money is.
3. **To win it all.** For some, a first-place result is their only ambition.

Realize that just finishing in the money in a large event is a victory to build on, and because it's a "short-term" situation, you will need a little "luck." You will need to survive at least one bad beat and put a bad beat on someone else along the way.

Implications of the Survival Mentality
In tournament play, your chips are finite. There is no never-ending supply as big as your bankroll. So your stack of chips becomes as precious as a canteen of water to a parched soul hopelessly lost in the desert. What does this mean to tournament play? Everything. Every decision to risk chips has far-reaching implications. And the fewer you have, the more valuable each one is. For you, yes, but your opponents are in the same desert. So you can use their fear in several ways.

First, when you bet, you will be less likely to be called. Therefore, you can open with worse hands than usual. (Most of your opponents will *not* open with worse hands than usual, but watch closely for those who do.) Second, if you *are* called, you can expect to be facing a better hand than normal. It generally takes a better hand to call than to bet in tournament poker. It follows that you don't really want to be called, nor do you want to just call the bets of others. You'd much prefer to be aggressive and win small pots or the blinds uncontested.

POKER POINTER

While they may be short-term odds-wise, these events can last all day and far into the night or even into several days. It follows that you need tremendous patience and stamina, in addition to your other poker skills. Discipline and serenity can move you into the money, even without good cards.

Third, you rarely want to be entering pots with two or more players already in. If you're going in, you always want the option of buying the pot right there. Fourth, survival means you will often lay down some very good hands, especially early in the tournament. And in no-limit, you want to avoid early coin-flip situations (such as a pair versus two overcards), unless you are one of the weaker players or are short-stacked (have very few chips left compared to the other players). *Position is extremely important, pot odds are much less so.* You want a clear advantage before you risk your chips, not a drawing hand—no matter how big the pot. You're not thinking long term here; tournaments are a short-term scenario.

What Kind of Tournament Is This?

Job one is finding out the payout, how many places are paid, rebuy policy, and when the tournament begins. With so many events being sold out these days, it pays to get there early! Sign up, and then check out and chat up the other entrants. Before devising strategy, you must be able to recognize the nature of the event. Some require great skill, while some take great luck. The key is how long the tournament will go. The longer it lasts, the bigger the edge for the better players, who have more time to use their skills. You can predict length by comparing the number of chips each player is given to the size of the initial blinds or antes and finding out how quickly the blinds/antes will be raised. If the blinds/antes are raised quickly (more often than every forty minutes), the event will be quicker—and chancier. If the blinds/antes are doubled at each level, that is a short tournament. If they only increase 50 percent or less, or if they are using a structure called "TEARS," that will be a longer event.

Play will start out fast in shorter events, so you cannot be as cautious. In longer events, you can be much more patient.

Rebuys and Add-Ons

Rebuys allow busted-out players to buy their way back into a tourney. Most lower buy-in events and super-satellites allow rebuys during the first three rounds if your chips fall below their initial level. At the end of the rebuy period, there is one last chance to up your stack, regardless of chip count, and that's called purchasing an "add-on." Most major events do not use rebuys or add-ons, but smaller events and most super-satellites do. Rebuy tournaments favor those with deep pockets.

It is important that you decide in advance how much money you're willing to invest in the tournament. First, be aware that 95 percent of the field will buy the add-on, so you will have to as well. As for rebuys, you want to set limits. It is foolish to go into a low-buy-in competition and then spend so much on rebuys that you could've entered a more significant event. Rebuying over and over is just throwing good money after bad. Your rebuy usually gives you an amount equal to your initial number of chips, but meanwhile, other players have doubled or tripled their stacks, so you are already an underdog. One or two rebuys and the add-on should be the max, and you should buy the add-on only if it doubles your stack or if you will own a below-average stack if you do not add on.

ASK JOHNNY QUADS

How does the House make money on tournaments?

Events are listed something like this: "$500 plus $50 No-Limit Hold'em." This means $500 goes to the prize pool, and $50 goes to the House. You will pay $550 when you sign up and are given a table and seat assignment. The House also makes money on all those players who hit the ring games after they bust out of the tournament.

The idea is to invest as little as possible. Let your opponents inflate the prize pool, not you. And if you are going to rebuy, don't wait until after you've gone all-in and lost. Rebuy as soon as you are eligible, so you have some power. Then if you get a hand, you can make some money with it.

The real tournament doesn't begin until players can no longer buy chips—when "death" is final—so during the rebuy period, strategy isn't much different from a standard ring game.

You have two things to watch for during the rebuy period. First, maniacs will be wildly building pots to quickly double their stacks if they get lucky, or going broke and rebuying if they don't. Second, some players will be trying to create a table image as either extremely tight or extremely loose-aggressive. Watch out for these players later if they try to use this image to play against type, with the maniac only playing rock-solid hands, and the tight player bluffing and stealing pots. Many players are loose early and tight late, but the opposite strategy might actually make more sense.

Chip Position and Stack Size

Playing chip position is one of the most important strategies in tournament poker. To survive, you must know how you stack up against the field and especially against the rest of your table. Find your position by dividing the number of remaining players into the total chips in the event, which will be posted. If you have more than this average, you're in the top half. If you're below the curve, you may have to loosen up a bit. Remember, winning small pots and stealing blinds and antes uncontested is a big part of tournament strategy, and you will find that players will not defend their blinds as often as in a ring game. Selective aggressiveness is rewarded—you need that second way to win (forcing others to fold) in every hand you're in. (The first way, of course, is having the best hand at the river.)

Big Stacks Versus Small Stacks

In tournaments, the big chip stacks have an edge, and the small ones are sweating it out. A big stack can bust a small one at any time in no-limit, but not vice versa. Small stacks must think twice about calling a big stack. Thus big stacks often can run over small stacks, but you can't be foolish with a big stack or you'll find yourself making those small stacks a lot bigger! A big stack gives you the comfort level to wait for premium hands and pick your spots to steal. Small stacks don't have that luxury. What you must avoid with a big stack is getting into big battles with other big stacks, especially late. Those big stacks can hurt you, so stay out of their way. Often, you can coast into the money if you don't get into a turf war with another giant. Don't get greedy. Let them come to you. Your goal is to get into the money, not win a certain number of pots.

POKER POINTER

If you are a short stack and the money cutoff line is nearing, don't focus on your own table. Get up and check out other tables for tiny stacks. How many are as desperate as you? Will they have to go all-in on their blinds soon? How many need to bust out before you finish in the money? This information is often the difference between being paid and getting nothing.

What to Do with a Small Stack

If you have a small stack, keep a close eye on your chips. If you have less than four times the big blind in limit or six times in no-limit or pot-limit, that is a small stack. If you get in dire straits, loosen up to maintain enough chips to ensure yourself that second way to win. If you cannot make an all-in bet that is at least a little scary in no-limit, or be able to bet through to the river in limit, others will call you down or put you all-in long before you have that big hand you're praying for.

There will come a time with a small stack when you will just have to go for it, but keep an eye on the blinds. Once they pass, you will be free and clear for another seven hands. If you are on the bubble (near the money), look for players with fewer chips than you. Can you outlast them without risking your stack? Watch the clock! Will the blinds increase soon? Can you make it to the paying spots without playing a hand?

ASK JOHNNY QUADS

On the World Poker Tour, why does a player hesitate so long with a hand he knows he's going to fold?

He wants to make his opponent sweat. Since this is an unpleasant experience, the opponent will be less likely to raise this player next time, especially if he is bluffing. The player also wants his foe to think he had a decent hand, not trash.

If you're the short stack, you have to gamble and play some hands, but don't be hasty. If it's crunch time, come in with a raise before you're down to just a few checks. You just want to isolate or buy the blinds/antes. You may have to go all-in on coin-flip hands like any pair, ace, or two face cards, and you want to do this before you get such a small stack that everyone can call you with impunity. The fewer the players, the more hands you will be forced to play.

If you are short-stacked, you will be forced to go all-in with any pair, ace-face or face-face hand and hope to buy the blinds or double up. And if you are one of the weaker players, you will be happy to get into any 50-50 "race" against a top player, such as a pair versus two overcards. On the other hand, if you are one of the top players, the last thing you want to do is to give a weak player a 50-50 shot at beating you, so be careful. Weaker players use this last fact to aggressively go all-in against players who think they are best. They will be reluctant to call you without a monster hand. But hesitate to call a top player's all-in bet. When you go all-in, you want the option of buying the pot outright without having to show a hand. You want uncontested pots in a tournament, not showdowns, and you won't get that by calling.

Tournament Tips
Try these strategy tips on for size:

- Winning a pot is more important than wringing a few extra bets out of someone. Take the sure thing.
- Don't go all-in against more than one player or if you believe you will have more than one caller.
- The players most likely to call an all-in bet are those with very large or extremely small ("desperate") stacks.
- Don't "get married" to a hand, no matter how good. If you're not desperate, don't take a big risk.

- When you're in cautious mode, try to see flops and fourth street in Stud cheaply in case your hand doesn't develop.
- Let others go to war. It's better for you to have one enemy with $50,000 than two with $25,000 apiece.
- Don't be afraid to go all-in in no-limit when you have top pair. You do not want the draws to get lucky.
- Heads-up, it's not about who has the best hand. It's about who doesn't have the worst hand.

Because a tournament is a short-term event, you will have to catch some cards to win, but don't be discouraged. Jack Strauss won the 1982 World Series of Poker after being down to his last chip! So don't throw in your final chips on a whim and a shrug. Fight to the end! Remember, like Jack, if you have "a chip and a chair," you're still in it.

CHAPTER 12

AS YOUR GAME EVOLVES

You won't be able to turn around without hearing something new about poker this year. And if tournaments receive corporate sponsorship, watch out! That extra money in the prize pool will lure fortune hunters like Blackbeard's treasure. How do you fit into the game's burgeoning future? Will you grow along with it? And how do you stand in that full-time gamble that is your life?

What to Do If You're Losing

Everyone suffers a first loss, and it's a tough one to swallow. But what if you've also suffered a second, a third, a fourth? You don't want to quit cold turkey, but you're losing a lot. Truthfully, there are some valid reasons to quit; losing consistently over several years, not improving, and/or not enjoying yourself being the main ones. You don't play poker to lose, but you don't have to give up. You can fight it. You start by asking some tough questions. Chief among them is whether you are playing just to be in action. Do you totally understand the game? Are you playing with scared money? Are you overrating your skills? Are the other players too skilled? Does it seem like other players always know your hand?

The most underestimated skill in poker is game selection—who you are playing against. Some games will never be profitable. Play against people you can beat, or don't bother. You're wasting time and money.

Take a hard look at yourself. Do you really understand what a good hand is in this game? In various situations? Are you acting, or just reacting? Are you putting pressure on, or are you just passive? Can you put someone on a hand, or are you lost and just playing your own cards? Can you discern what a foe thinks you have, and when he bets, what he thinks of his own hand? Can you smoke out when someone is overvaluing a hand?

Are you a predictable "book player"? Regulars can spot these types a mile away. These rigid, conservative players are not the forceful table presence they need to be. *This* book, it is hoped, will move you beyond the "book player" level.

Tips to Turn Things Around
If you're losing on a consistent basis, follow these tips to get back in the game:

- Ask other players for advice. Pay a pro if you have to.
- Vary your playing style. Get out of the rut.

- Try a new variation, venue, stakes, and/or players.
- Seek out a game with weaker players and loose action.
- Keep the expert, aggressive players on your right.
- Don't look for reasons to call. Look for reasons to fold.
- Don't play a hand unless you can bet aggressively.
- Play the players. Are you analyzing and adjusting to your foes?
- In general, only bluff until you are caught, then tighten up.
- Cultivate a table image the opposite of the way you are playing.
- If you can't decide between a tight or wild image, choose wild.
- Don't call a bet on the river when you know you are beat.

Most of all, don't give up. You don't have to be an expert to win, just better than your opponents. Try some new things, like the strategies in this book, and tighten up until you find the problem, because playing too many starting hands and staying with them too long are the most serious mistakes in poker. In most cases, the best course is to just play straightforwardly—fold with a bad hand, bet with a good hand. Don't overdo the fancy plays. If you get ahead, quit early and go home a winner.

Forget the Battles, Win the War

You know that every poker hand is a skirmish in a larger battle—the game you're in. But each game is part of an even larger picture: the war. The war is your total poker experience. You win a game when you walk away with more money than you came with, but how do you win the war? If you decide that you will never play poker again, that for one reason or another you are through with it (for many, this won't be until they move on to that big casino in the sky), *and you're ahead,* then you are victorious. You have won the battle of poker and defeated your foes. You are quitting "winners."

But there is more to it than money. Poker would be a lonely pastime if money was all it was, as well as a waste of a lot of hours (unless you're earning a really good living at it). You are a winner at poker if it has been an enriching experience, if it has made you a better person, if you have met friends, acquaintances, and characters, gained knowledge, and stayed sharp and focused. If it has brought the thrill of competition and joy to your life, and if you have brought joy to others around the green felt (by some method other than by giving them your chips), then you are a winner.

POKER POINTER

"Every conscious act requires risk. Every conscious act requires decision. Put these two facts together and you realize that the secret to life is not to avoid gambling, but to gamble well."—*Author/lecturer/ pro Mike Caro*

To maximize your profits, you take no prisoners when you have a winning hand. But the same goes for your game as a whole. When you've "got game," you make more money by going up in stakes. If you start out playing $3–$6 or $4–$8

Hold'em or $2–$10 Stud—and you should not start lower—your goal is not to stay there. Your objective is to move up. If you are a winner and move from $4–$8 to $8–$16, you have doubled your stakes and your possible profit—if you can play the same style.

The question is whether you can adapt. You must be able to play with the same fearlessness and strength at the elevated level, because higher-limit players will try to intimidate you if they feel you're moving up. They know *they* can handle the pressure, but you'll have to prove that *you* can.

Love the Game

Your two missions at the table (winning money and having fun) are really one. If you are having fun, you will probably be winning, and if you are winning, you will definitely be

Another great way to get back on top of your game is to keep records. Smart players keep three types:

- **Wins and losses**. Of course, you keep these so you can see exactly where you stand. It is too easy to deceive yourself when relying on memory. Track the type of game, stakes, venue, time at the table, and amount, with comments.

- **Your calls**. When you have a tough decision at the river and you call, keep track of whether you won or lost. You should win if you're in at the river. If you lose more than 25 percent, you call too much.

- **The players**. Keep a notebook of opponents with their tendencies, how they play hands, loose or tight, bluffs, tells, skill level—anything. Talk to your tablemates; they'll be happy to fill you in.

having fun. It all comes down to loving the game: If you don't love poker, you will not win.

The more skilled you become, the more money (and fun) will flow your way, because in poker, unlike golf, pool, and other sports, there is no handicap. Players of all levels compete one-on-one. Poker players all think they're unbeatable, and you can use this overconfidence to win and achieve your goal of being "your own casino" with a built-in edge on every hand.

Remember, the more hands you play, the less deviation from the norm you can expect. This is why everyday players watch the odds so closely. They seek to minimize the deviation (luck) and make their long-term results predictable. But no matter how many hands they play, there is always the chance that at any given moment—or even in the long term—something "crazy" could happen. This is what makes the game so timeless and exciting.

As you read the final lines of this book, remember that you're only at the start of your lifelong poker journey. You have enough knowledge to give it a try. The only missing piece is experience. So get out there and find out what's in the cards for you!

INDEX